Charles and Diana

Also by Penny Junor

Diana, Princess of Wales
Charles
Margaret Thatcher
Babyware
Burton

PENNY JUNOR

Charles and Diana

Portrait of a Marriage

Photographs by
Jayne Fincher

HEADLINE

First published in 1991
by HEADLINE BOOK PUBLISHING PLC

10 9 8 7 6 5 4 3 2 1

British Library Cataloguing in Publication Data

Junor, Penny
    Charles and Diana : portrait of a marriage.
    1. Great Britain. Charles, Prince of Wales, Interpersonal
relationships with Diana, Princess of Wales
    I. Title
    941.0850922

    ISBN 0–7472–0350–4

Typeset in 11½ / 13 pt Symposia
by Colset Private Limited, Singapore

Designed by John Hawkins

Colour Reproduction by Hilo Offset Ltd,
Telford Way, Colchester, Essex, CO4 4QP

Printed and bound in Great Britain by
Richard Clay Ltd, Bungay, Suffolk

HEADLINE BOOK PUBLISHING PLC
Headline House
79 Great Titchfield Street
London W1P 7FN

For
Sam, Alex, Jack and Peta

Contents

Author's Note and Acknowledgements

Towards the end of last year I was asked on Radio 4's *Today* programme whether I thought the marriage was in trouble. The Prince had just returned to public duties after four months off with his broken arm. He had spent much of that time apart from his wife and children. He seemed bad-tempered and out of sorts. What was the problem? Wasn't he neglecting his family? I said that in spite of the long period apart, no. Their marriage was actually very healthy, and if he was looking grumpy it was because the press had been so intrusive.

I was immediately telephoned by a journalist who said I was out of step with the rest of the media. What evidence did I have for saying this?

My evidence is in the following pages. It comes from talking to some of the people closest to both the Prince and Princess, including some friends, some relatives and many of the people directly involved in their working lives.

This was not my conclusion five years ago when I wrote a biography of Prince Charles. I said that his marriage was not a very happy one, and at that time I believe I was right; but a lot has happened in the last five years. The Prince and Princess have grown and developed, and their situation has changed. The problem now is that the media has not yet caught up with that change.

Since many of the people that have helped me draw my conclusions have to remain anonymous, I will not single out anyone by name, but simply say many many thanks to them all for being so generous with their time and expertise. What becomes very quickly apparent when meeting the people closely associated with the Prince and Princess of Wales is that they have remarkably nice people around them, all of whom seem to have a great sense of humour. I am not sure whether that is cause or effect, but it makes dealing with them an enormous pleasure.

Special thanks also to those of them who read and checked the manuscript, and helped weed out inaccuracies.

The book is made, of course, by the photographs, all of which came from Jayne Fincher, who has been a joy to work with. I am enormously grateful to her for giving me the run of her files and the hours she devoted to finding such perfect pictures for the text.

I should also say thank you to Alan Brooke at Headline, for the idea, for his encouragement and enthusiasm; and to Dasha Shenkman, my agent, for her unfailing support; also to Linda Collins for all her help.

My family, as usual, have been neglected but totally marvellous.

The family together at Highgrove as Charles approached his 40th birthday

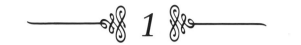

1

The Wedding of the Century

No marriage has had the exposure of this one. It was the wedding of the century, the fairy tale that excited, fired and fascinated people all over the world. Millions poured on to the streets of London on 29 July 1981 to be able to say they were there on the day, to tell their children and grandchildren what it was like. Hundreds of millions more watched it on television and can remember the dress she wore, the horse-drawn carriage she arrived in, the kiss on the balcony of Buckingham Palace, the cheering, the music, the colour and the happiness.

For Lady Diana Spencer, just twenty years old, it was the most thrilling day of her life. She walked down the long red-carpeted aisle of St Paul's Cathedral a commoner. She returned a princess. It was all her dreams come true. She had married her Prince, the man she loved. They would have beautiful children and live happily ever after.

But it was not quite so simple. As she took her wedding vows, Diana was saying goodbye to the life that she had taken for granted for twenty years. Saying goodbye to the freedom to walk down a street on her own, to browse through the sales, to decide on the spur of the moment to visit friends, or meet for a drink in the pub. She had married not just the man, she had married his job, and all that it involved. She had married a man for whom duty always came first. She had married a large, closely knit family. Worse still, she had married into a life so public that at times she felt there was no place on earth where she could escape from the prying eyes.

The Prince had high hopes on that July day too. He had spoken earnestly, some years before, about finding the right girl to marry, about not letting his head be ruled by his heart; but come the day, he had married because he had fallen in love. At the age of thirty-three, he had found someone to share his life and passions with; someone to help shoulder the burden. Someone pretty, witty and sexy, who made him laugh and feel young and carefree.

But it was not to be quite as he had hoped either. Their ten years of marriage have been fraught with difficulties that neither could have foreseen. They have had to learn to live with one another, to adjust, to get used to each other's habits, hobbies,

29 July 1981. Newly married, Charles and Diana on the steps of St Paul's Cathedral

friends and relations – the most crucial and critical period for every newly married couple – but they have had to do it all under the full glare of the media. Every step, every look, every word has been quoted, scrutinized and analysed. They have been spied on by the paparazzi, betrayed by trusted servants, embarrassed by indiscreet friends, and have had to endure a constant torrent of innuendo, gossip, lies and half-truths in newspapers, magazines and books – none of which are they able to repudiate.

At times it has looked as though the difficulties might have proved insurmountable, the strain too much. The media seemed to be willing the marriage to fall to pieces. The adulation that had greeted Diana in the early days began to turn sour. 'Revelations' from a bitter ex-valet branded her a tyrant with a heated temper who had swept into the Prince's life and, like a spoilt child, banished trusted staff and old friends and even stopped the Prince from hunting and shooting. Charles, said journalists 'in the know', was being 'pussy whipped' by a petulant and jealous wife.

Any attempt to redress the situation backfired. The couple invited newspaper editors to a series of private lunches at Kensington Palace, to appeal to their better nature, but to no avail. The editors revelled in the honour, ate their lunches and went back to their offices to continue publishing every last tit-bit they could find. The Prince and Princess allowed the television cameras into their home, so the public could see for themselves that they were a close and happy family. After a hour of simpering sycophancy from the presenter, the Prince took the viewer into his garden, where he said he loved to sit and think and talk to his plants. That was it. The loony Prince. Every time he tried to make any kind of serious statement or speech for years thereafter, people came back to the plants.

They were worrying times. Diana took the criticism to heart, avidly read what was being said about her and became depressed and despondent. Charles worried about the effect it was having on her; and grew angry and frustrated on his own behalf, that no one seemed interested in the ills of the world. All they wanted to do was poke fun at him, look at the cut of his suit, or his hairstyle, or measure his bald patch.

Ten years on, however, Charles and Diana have come through it. They have found a new enthusiasm for life, a new determination to be the people they are and behave as they will. They have settled down, sorted out their personal problems, adjusted their lives to accommodate each other, found a way to cope with the pressure and emerged with a very strong successful partnership.

Furthermore, the strength they have built into their marriage has brought confidence to them both. Diana has made the transition from girl to woman and has become secure and fulfilled; Charles has confronted the spectre of middle age and doubt, and emerged certain. He has not just found a role for himself, which was something he had agonized over for years, but has used his position to lead an assault on the ills of modern society; to try to alter people's basic thinking, not just in an effort to improve their lives, but to persuade them of the need to preserve the planet for future generations. After years of being thought a crank, he is at last being taken

1990 in Hungary. Ten years on their problems are behind them

seriously. Where once he felt like giving up, he now has the zeal and determination to push further and harder and keep on going until there is real change in the way mankind behaves.

The Prince's contribution is unique. It is unlike that of any politician, environmentalist or businessman, however committed and well intentioned they may be. He has taken up the challenge to lead. He no longer simply makes meaningful speeches that stir things up. He believes we are at a deeply significant turning point in human history and if we are to come through it we have to change not just the way people behave, but also the way in which they think. He is convinced we have to adopt entirely new value systems, change our philosophical orientation and spiritual thinking; stop behaving as though the earth is here for mankind's personal convenience and learn to regard ourselves as one small part of a much larger whole.

He knows precisely where he is going now and is fit and eager for the challenge. He no longer fears ridicule or criticism; instead, his fear is that people will not act swiftly enough, that human nature has locked itself into a process of acquisitiveness and materialism, and that three hundred years of our industrial society have alienated people from the aesthetic values mankind once possessed.

These are his own thoughts; the Prince is nobody's puppet. The press scoffed at his walks in the Kalahari Desert, at his fascination with lost and ancient tribes; but experiences like that, plus a lifetime of travelling all over the world, seeing underdeveloped and overdeveloped countries and every kind of political regime, has brought him to this viewpoint. Time and again he is savaged for speaking on subjects about which his critics claim he knows nothing. In fact, his education is encyclopaedic and eclectic. He reads and digests material on a vast range of topics and picks the brains of most of the leading authorities. He trawls for advice and information from dozens of people, who find themselves invited to Kensington Palace quite out of the blue.

The Princess has her own area of interest. Her concerns are much closer to home, much more for people and individuals than cosmic matters, which provides a perfect foil for her husband. She has spent much of the last ten years establishing herself and securing her home base, and it is only now that she is beginning to realize her potential. She has grown into an elegant and gracious woman, but lost none of the spark that made her such an endearing young bride. She wins hearts everywhere she goes, and, with a quick aside, puts everyone instantly and skilfully at their ease. She also goes anywhere she wants. She has emerged as independent, resourceful and resilient. With no qualifications and precious little experience, she has taken on the job of Princess of Wales and is turning it into a significant career – and at the same time has brought up two small boys.

Five years ago people might have thought her greatest contribution had been to the British fashion industry. No longer. She has turned into a champion of the underdog, gone out on a limb to support unglamorous causes like AIDS victims, drug abusers and the mentally handicapped. She has worked tirelessly and helped raise millions of

Diana wins hearts everywhere she goes

pounds for the charities she has taken on. She is now growing into a confident speaker, prepared to say what she thinks. Whereas once her every outfit hit the headlines, it is now her every word – and they are very much her words. In this respect, she has learnt a great deal from her husband. Like the Prince, she requests and gathers together information and reading material on all of the subjects she has taken on. People who meet her in the course of a briefing or a visit are constantly surprised by her knowledge, the intelligence of her questions, and her retention of what she has read – often on quite scientific subjects. Added to that is her instinctive feeling for people – what to do and say that will please them most. She is in the good news business and a master of the art.

Between them, the Waleses have established a way of operating over the last ten years that is unmistakably their own; and quite unlike any other branch of the Royal Family. Their homes, both in London and in the country, epitomize their attitude. They are comfortable, friendly, lived-in places; elegant, not grand. The furnishings are pretty, a mixture of modern and antique, and the rooms are full of light and colour, with large vases of flowers and pot plants liberally scattered about. Children and dogs run around and climb on the furniture. Their sons are noisy and mischievous and don't always do what they are told, and in every respect are normal, healthy, confident little boys. There is formality when there has to be, but everyone who visits either house is immediately put at ease.

They have achieved the same in the way they work. Traditionally, members of the Royal Family play a passive role. Wherever they go they are escorted by a vast armada of local dignitaries, including the Lord Lieutenant, the Mayor or Mayoress, complete with the chains of office, the Chief Constable of Police and every last member of the town council. This mass of people, all dressed in their Sunday best, bedecked with badges and brass, hovers like a human shield, while the Royal in question inspects whatever is on show, shakes a few select hands and exchanges benign pleasantries, before being whisked away in a grand black limousine. The Prince and Princess have each, in their own way, reversed the order of play. They deal with the dignitaries in the politest possible way, but it is clear to everyone that it is not the dignitaries they have

Washington D.C. 1986, with Vice-President and Mrs Bush. Charles has taught Diana how to handle state occasions

come to see and talk to, but the ordinary people. They very swiftly get down to basics, ask pertinent questions, build up a rapport, and do so away from the rest of the party, away from the reporters and press cameras. This is where they do such good, where they really make a visit worth while and where they learn what ordinary people think, need and feel.

They are very much a two-career couple and, although the work overlaps from time to time, they have two very distinct careers, which take them in different directions. Diana has learnt a phenomenal amount in the last ten years – much of it from her husband. He has taught her how to handle state occasions, how to deal with foreign potentates, when to speak and when not to, how to manage tiring tours and how to cope with the strains of travel. He has helped her with her public speaking, suggested ideas, discussed her concerns and boosted her confidence when it was low. Diana has helped Charles by bringing him into the modern era, teasing him and leavening his spirits, and keeping him young and abreast of young people's thinking. She too has given him confidence and relieved some of the loneliness of his position.

It is a successful and formidable double-act. They may not have found quite the soulmate in each other that they had been looking for, but their relationship has made up for it in other ways. It is now a caring and loving one, in which they both feel free to be themselves, and the trust between them is absolute. They are still irritated and frustrated when their privacy is invaded and still upset by hurtful articles in the press, or inaccurate stories. They argue from time to time, they get tired and cross and let stress get the better of them, like any other couple, but the union is essentially a happy one. Against all the odds it has worked, and this is a measure of just how strong they both were as individuals when they came to the marriage ten years ago.

Their union has not only survived the rigours of a decade, but has come out at the other end stronger than ever. It is that strength, both individually and collectively, that will ensure that if the monarchy survives into the twenty-first century, it will not just be as 'a privileged irrelevance', but as a very potent force for good.

A Love Match

It was a love match. Despite all the scheming and matchmaking that went on behind the scenes, when Charles and Diana took their wedding vows on 29 July 1981, they were undoubtedly in love.

Diana had been in love with Prince Charles for several years, since their first meeting when she was a sixteen-year-old home from school for half-term and he was her elder sister's boyfriend. He had come to Althorp, their family home, for a pheasant shoot. He later said his first impression of her then had been, 'What a very jolly and amusing and attractive sixteen-year-old. I mean great fun – bouncy and full of life and everything.' In truth, he was very much smitten by Sarah at the time and he would scarcely have noticed the rather nondescript little sister who fell passionately in love that day.

That was November 1977. It was the year of the Queen's Silver Jubilee and the Prince, just twenty-nine, was drawing to the end of his first year as a full-time working member of the 'family firm'. He had been through school and university, he had travelled the world, he had completed five years in the armed forces, he had flown fighter planes and helicopters – and for nine months had had command of a mine hunter in the North Sea.

On the romantic front he had had a string of engaging and pretty girlfriends, not least of all the vivacious flame-haired Lady Sarah Spencer. He had been in and out of love, but never found quite the right girl at quite the right time to make him a wife.

Diana was nothing more than a schoolgirl, unworldly in the extreme. She was popular with the other girls at West Heath and enjoyed her years there, but she was never very promising academically, and her reading was almost entirely limited to Barbara Cartland romantic novels. Outside the classroom she fared better. She consistently won swimming cups and also the school dancing competition one year. She took up the piano and, according to her headmistress Ruth Rudge, 'made phenomenal progress for someone who started late'; and although she never made it into any of the school teams, she loved tennis. During her last year she joined the Voluntary Service Unit and visited an old lady in Sevenoaks once a week. None of it was remarkable, but it all added up. In her last term she won the Miss Clark Lawrence Award for service to the school: a special award, not necessarily given, 'for

Diana, pulling faces, was still the girl he remembered, great fun, bouncy and full of life

anyone who has done things that otherwise might have gone unsung'.

After meeting Prince Charles, Diana went back to school that November day to have a second shot at her O levels, which eluded her yet again, and the following month, at the age of sixteen and a half, she left for good. Next stop was finishing school in Switzerland, where speaking English was a punishable offence. In theory, she studied domestic science – dressmaking and cooking – and took a Pitman's correspondence and typing course. In practice, she learnt to ski; but it was the first time she had been away from her friends and family, the first time she had been on a plane, the first time she had been abroad, and she was desperately unhappy. After just six weeks she returned home and refused to go back.

By the time she and the Prince were engaged two years later, she was still no better educated. She had been a mother's help to a family in Hampshire, she had babysat through an agency in London, and had taken on cleaning jobs. She had done a three-month cookery course and, as a last-ditch attempt to acquire some proper qualifications, she had enrolled as a student teacher with Betty Vacani, in Knights-bridge, who ran dancing classes for tiny tots. This had not worked either. Finally, in the autumn of 1979, Diana found the perfect job, working part-time as an assistant in a small kindergarten in Pimlico, for a friend of her other sister, Jane. It left plenty of time for shopping and meeting friends, two of her passions.

Unlike the Prince, she had had no love affairs when their friendship began at the beginning of that year. She had a wide circle of friends, all from the same social set, ex-public school, most of them with parents living in the country. She had her own flat, at Coleherne Court off the Old Brompton Road – bought with money that had been put into trust until her eighteenth birthday – which she shared with girlfriends. It was prettily furnished by Diana and, although the hallway was a jumble of bicycles and tennis racquets, the rest of the flat was remarkably clean and neat. Diana could never go to bed and leave a mess behind, however late; she would always tidy up and wash any dirty dishes. Diana and her friends were a clean-living set – none of them smoked or drank much – and when they went out, it tended to be in a group. They would go to one another's flats, have supper in a bistro, go to a film, or sit at home with bowls of spaghetti, chatting and watching television. At weekends they would go off to the country.

Within her own social set, Diana was confident and happy. She was quite unso-phisticated, but always good company at a dinner party, guaranteed to get everyone talking and laughing. She was fun, and people liked to have her around because she was easy and undemanding and always had a quick reply. But she was no intellectual and, apart from a passion for the ballet, which she used to attend with her grand-mother, Ruth, Lady Fermoy, she was like any ordinary teenager. She spent her time shopping, reading women's magazines, listening to pop music and watching television.

On the face of it, she and Prince Charles had very little in common when they re-met in 1979. Quite apart from the intellectual and educational differences, they did not even share the same hobbies. Charles was a compulsive horseman; Diana didn't ride. The Prince loved opera; her love was ballet. He hated pop music; she enjoyed it. Her sport was tennis; he had never played. For this reason, some of the Prince's closest friends were against the marriage; they feared that with so little in common it could never work.

But there was more to Diana Spencer than met the eye. Beneath the giggling, bubbly little-girl exterior was strength and depth; an uncanny maturity and a sensitivity that belied her years. For all her privilege and wealth, life had not been easy and the experiences of childhood had left an indelible mark.

Diana's parents had had an unhappy marriage. Her father, Earl Spencer, at that time Viscount Althorp, was the perfect gentleman to all who knew him, but not so gentlemanly behind closed doors. Her mother, Frances, stayed with him until she had produced the son he so desperately wanted, but when Diana was just six years old her mother left home. She had met and fallen in love with Peter Shand Kydd, a wallpaper millionaire, seen a chance of happiness, and taken it. What she had not known was that in leaving home she would have to forfeit her four children. There was a messy divorce and, in the subsequent custody proceedings, custody of Sarah, Jane, Diana and Charles was granted to their father. Johnnie Spencer had called upon some of the highest names in the land as character witnesses, including his ex-wife's own mother, Ruth, Lady Fermoy.

Of all the children, Diana was the most affected by the sudden loss of her mother. The two older girls had already begun boarding school, so were away for most of the time, and Charles was only three and easily amused by the nanny. It was Diana, aged six – old enough to understand she had been left, but not yet old enough to understand why – who felt so bereft. The security she had known was suddenly gone, her small world shattered.

During that period everyone rallied round, particularly her two grandmothers, Ruth, Lady Fermoy and Cynthia, Countess Spencer. She became close to both women and, although she still saw her mother from time to time and still has a very strong relationship

Diana with her mother, Frances Shand Kydd. The marriage to Earl Spencer had not been a happy one

with her that has not been diminished by the divorce, a special bond was forged with the two older women. When Countess Spencer died in 1972, it was another loss for Diana to cope with.

Prince Charles had had similar experiences. His grandmother had been like a mother to him for most of his childhood. Obviously there was no broken family in his case, but his mother was always either busy or away, even before she became Queen, and her parents stepped into the breach. It was his grandparents he spent his first Christmas with. He was with them again for his second Christmas and his third birthday. He was even with them the night the King died in 1952. It was his grandmother he spent his fifth birthday with and that same year his parents went off on a tour of the Commonwealth, which took them away from him for six long months. To the small child standing on the dockside waving goodbye it was a minor bereavement every time. As a result, Charles is closer to his grandmother in many ways than his own mother. Diana, likewise.

The Prince and Princess's grandmothers have been the best of friends for most of their lives. Ruth, Lady Fermoy and her husband Maurice knew the Queen Mother and King George VI when they were still Duke and Duchess of York, before the abdication. They remained friends and, when Maurice Fermoy died in 1952, Ruth became the Queen Mother's lady-in-waiting. There is no doubt that the two old ladies did a little plotting to marry their favourite grandchildren off to one another; but without the events of 1979 their dearest hopes might never have come to be.

There is no doubt the Queen Mother did a little plotting

If the Queen Mother provided a mother figure for Charles, it was his great-uncle, Lord Mountbatten, who became a father substitute. His own father, Prince Philip, was in the Navy for much of his childhood and the relationship between father and son was in any event a difficult one. Prince Philip was frankly disappointed in his first born and took no pains to hide his feelings. Charles was too sensitive for his liking, too intellectual, too philosophical, and although Charles adored his father and has spent a lifetime trying to please him and be as he would like, he has never really succeeded. As a result, he grew up with very little self-confidence. There is no doubt that Charles has done a great deal that his father has been proud of and has excelled at sports like polo that the Duke of Edinburgh played when he was younger, but the Prince never felt he was good enough.

Charles with Lord Mountbatten in 1976 – a vital figure in his life

In his wisdom, Lord Mountbatten saw what was happening and, after his retirement in 1965, concentrated his attention on the young Prince and became a vital figure in his life. Charles adored him and had done since he was a small child. Uncle Dickie, as he was known to the whole family, was a dynamic, tyrannical figure, full of energy, drive and ambition, who aroused strong passions in everyone who came into contact with him. He was a national hero, he had been Supreme Commander in South East Asia during the Second World War, the last Viceroy and first Governor General of India, First Sea Lord, and finally Chief of the Defence Staff. Born in 1900, the same year as the Queen Mother, he had spent twenty-three years at the top, he had travelled all over the world, he had stories and memories of escapades and people and was a colourful raconteur.

To Charles he was an indispensable source of wisdom and experience and he relished the time spent in his company. Mountbatten saw Charles for what he was and liked what he saw, and for the first time the growing Prince was given some real sense of his own worth. His great-uncle took Charles under his wing and prepared him for the job ahead. No one could have been better suited for the role, nor taken to it with more enthusiasm. He became friend, teacher, mentor and confidant. Charles spent many a weekend with Mountbatten at Broadlands, his home in Hampshire, where he felt totally at ease. The Prince took his problems to Broadlands and also his girlfriends. It provided the perfect sanctuary and Mountbatten was always there with time and interest to talk and advise.

By 1971, however, Charles was in the Navy and much of his time was spent at sea. 'As you know only too well,' he wrote after leaving Broadlands on one occasion to embark on a six-month cruise, 'to me it has become a second home in so many ways, and no one could ever have had such a splendid honorary grandpapa in the history of avuncular relationships.' The affection was entirely reciprocated. Mountbatten missed Charles enormously when he went off on long trips and felt lonely and deprived without his increasingly regular visits. 'I've been thinking of you – far more', he wrote, 'than I had ever expected to think of a young man – but then I've got to know you so well, I really miss you very much.' And in his diary he wrote, 'It's lovely having him here, we've had so many cosy talks. What a really charming young man he is.'

The advice that came out of those cosy talks, however, was not necessarily heeded. On one occasion, for example, Charles flew down to Broadlands to consult Mountbatten about a speech he had written for the Gandhi centenary tribute. The older man read the text overnight and came up with some suggested changes, all of which the Prince ignored. 'He very politely pointed out in each case,' recalled Mountbatten, 'that it was not the way he would have phrased it, and so it remained virtually unchanged. I thought it was really splendid.'

But on the subject of women, the Prince did take his honorary grandfather's advice. 'I believe, in a case like yours,' wrote Mountbatten, coincidentally on St Valentine's Day in 1974, 'the man should sow his wild oats and have as many affairs as he can before settling down, but for a wife he should choose a suitable, attractive and sweet-charactered girl *before* she met anyone else she might fall for. I think it is disturbing for women to have experiences if they have to remain on a pedestal after marriage.'

As fast as the Prince could comply, however, the press were trying to marry him off. 'I've only got to look twice at someone,' he said in desperation, 'and the next morning I'm engaged to her.'

It was not only intensely irritating, but it also frightened many women off, and made the normal process of two people getting to know one another quite impossible. Thus having Broadlands to use for this purpose made life very much easier. While happy to welcome any number of beautiful women to his home, Lord Mountbatten secretly cherished hopes that Charles would marry his granddaughter, Amanda Knatchbull, and by 1979 was busy plotting ways of bringing them together.

A visit to India being planned for the Prince the following year seemed the perfect opportunity. Mountbatten proposed that he and Amanda should accompany Charles, so he could show 'the two young people I love so much . . . the country which means so much to me', but the Duke of Edinburgh thought this a bad idea. He thought it a mistake for the Prince to make his first visit in the shadow of such a legendary figure. David Checketts, who was Prince Charles's private secretary at the time, was also dubious. 'You think I'll take over the whole show, don't you?' accused Mountbatten.

However, terrorists determined the issue. On 27 August 1979 Lord Mountbatten, on holiday in County Sligo in the Republic of Ireland, was brutally murdered. A fifty-pound bomb, planted in his fishing boat, exploded as he set off out of the little harbour of Mullaghmore to inspect lobster pots. He had with him his daughter and her husband, Lord and Lady Brabourne, their fourteen-year-old twin sons, Nicholas and Timothy Knatchbull, Lord Brabourne's elderly mother, and Paul Maxwell, a local lad who enjoyed helping with the boat. Miraculously, Lord and Lady Brabourne and one son, Timothy, survived. Lady Brabourne senior was pulled out of the water alive, but died in hospital the next day. The rest of the fishing party were killed.

Mountbatten's 'execution', claimed the IRA faction responsible, 'was a way of bringing emotionally home to the English ruling-class and its working-class slaves . . . that their government's war on us is going to cost them as well . . . We will tear out their sentimental imperialist heart.'

Many hearts were torn out that day, among them the Prince's. He was in Iceland, fishing with friends, when he heard the news and flew straight to Windsor Castle, to a father who was still unable to help. Charles was overcome with grief; he felt shocked, frightened and alone. He had lost the greatest friend he would ever have. He had lost the one person who believed in him, the one person whom he could trust with his innermost thoughts. Life, as he told his friends, would never be the same again.

Any prospect of romance with Amanda Knatchbull was killed that day too. But in the weeks that followed they became very close and clung to one another in their loss. After the funeral Charles retreated to Balmoral, where he watched the BBC obituary of Mountbatten over and over again, and walked the lonely moors. He was joined there by Amanda's brother, Norton (now Lord Romsey), and his fiancée, Penelope Eastwood; and although the cousins had never been especially friendly before, a strong bond grew between them as they talked day after day, trying to make sense of it all.

A year before his death, Charles had written to Lord Mountbatten, once again thanking him for his help. 'I was deeply grateful for our conversation yesterday morning and being able to pick your brains on the subjects was an *immense* help. As I said to you yesterday, I have no idea what we shall do without you when you finally decide to depart. It doesn't bear thinking about, but I only hope I shall have learnt *something* from you in order to carry it on in some way or another.'

3

'For God's Sake, Ring Me Up – I'm Going to Need You'

Had Lord Mountbatten lived, there is a good chance that Diana Spencer would not have become Princess of Wales. He might have foreseen the problems that would ensue after their marriage, seen that there was a gulf between Charles and Diana that would be difficult to bridge and advised against it. But Mountbatten was gone and no one would ever quite fill the void he left.

His death quite literally shattered the Prince and for a time he lost all sense of purpose. While Mountbatten was still alive, Charles had begun working on many projects and had become enthused by what he could do to help the young and the disadvantaged; he was fired by what needed to be done in the inner cities and keen to find ways of defusing racial tension. Some of his staff disapproved of the direction he was taking, and four months before Mountbatten died, his private secretary, Sir David Checketts, resigned. He was replaced by an even greater traditionalist, Edward Adeane, who also had reservations about what the Prince was doing. But Mountbatten had backed up Charles. He more than anyone appreciated that if the monarchy was to survive, it needed to be updated. It could not afford to be seen as a drain on the taxpayer and it should be relevant to the times.

After Mountbatten's death, Charles no longer knew where he was going. He grew withdrawn and introspective. Help came from a number of sources, including his own deep faith, but there were individuals too. The Queen Mother was one. She understood his grief and his sense of loss and loneliness – she had been there herself, after the King's death – and she knew about the feelings of despair and the long, long time the scars would take to heal, but she also knew about the importance of carrying on.

Another source of support was Sir Laurens van der Post, who had also known Mountbatten, and who had been a Japanese prisoner of war in Java. This extraordi-

Had Mountbatten lived, Diana may never have become Princess of Wales.
Rumours of a royal romance were rife in November 1980

nary man, explorer, farmer, writer and mystic, taught Charles to seek the depth and strength within himself, to use the experience of Mountbatten's death, to use the suffering and learn from it: to grow in the spiritual sense; and above all, to ensure that his great-uncle had not died in vain.

Charles rallied. The year before Mountbatten died he had taken over the reins of the United World Colleges (UWC) from his great-uncle. This movement, co-founded with Kurt Hahn, founder of Gordonstoun, was a passion of Mountbatten. Its aim was to promote peace and international understanding through education. Lord Mountbatten had spent ten years tirelessly promoting the dream, talking about it all over the world, often in the highest places, inspiring everyone around him and shamelessly raising money to build more colleges. At the end of his ten years there were three: in Canada, Singapore, and the original one, Atlantic College in Wales. Charles had taken over the role of president determined to make a positive contribution.

Van der Post reminded Charles that to slow down, even for a while, would be to give the terrorists what they had wanted. The Prince knew his friend was right. He had had 2,500 letters from members of the public expressing their grief, sympathy and admiration for a man who they felt had in some way belonged to ordinary people and understood them. Charles knew he had to fight for them. Mountbatten had wanted him to be a leader of men. Now was the time to do it.

The Prince had come to know van der Post in Kenya two years before, when he had been his guide on safari. He is a remarkable old man in any setting, but in the bushveld of southern Africa, where he was born and has lived for much of his life, he was in his element. Every evening the small party would sit under the stars and listen to his stories of life in the African interior, his extensive travels and explorations, his war years and his friendship with the Swiss psychologist Carl Jung. The Prince felt he was in the company of someone very special, took great delight in time spent talking to him, and was inspired by all that he heard. Guided by his new-found friend, Charles studied Jung and also the work of economist and philosopher E. F. Schumacher, who wrote a book entitled *Small Is Beautiful*; over the years the Prince has found many of the answers he was searching for.

Charles put on a brave face to the world, but secretly he was in turmoil for many, many months; and one other person who helped see him through this period was Diana.

They had re-met, after that first encounter at Althorp, at Sandringham in January 1979, when the Queen had invited Diana and her sister Sarah (whose relationship with the Prince was well and truly over) for a weekend's shooting. It was not a surprising invitation. Their other sister, Jane, had married Robert Fellowes, a member of the Queen's permanent staff, the year before; and, given the rest of the Spencer family's connections with the Royal Family, the surprise was that she had never been invited before. Both of her grandmothers had been ladies-in-waiting to the Queen Mother. Her father had been an equerry to the Queen and to King George VI before

Diana with her father. No one had expected him to survive a massive cerebral haemorrhage

that; and before her grandfather died in 1975 and her father became the Eighth Earl Spencer and moved to Althorp, the family had lived in a house on the Sandringham Estate. It was where Diana was born and had spent the first fourteen years of her life.

Diana arrived at Sandringham that weekend having just been through a most traumatic period. Her father, whom she adored, had collapsed the previous September with a cerebral haemorrhage and had lain in a coma in the National Hospital in Queen Square, London, for nearly four months. No one expected him to live. To make matters worse, he had a new wife, Raine, formerly Lady Dartmouth, a formidable woman who became fiercely protective. She set up a bedside vigil, had special drugs imported from Germany, played him his favourite music and discouraged everyone else from visiting, including his own children. Her steely determination, however, had worked, and that very weekend Earl Spencer had been released from hospital and moved into a suite at the Dorchester Hotel, until he was strong enough to be moved home to Northamptonshire. It had been a difficult time for everyone, but especially Diana, who was perhaps closest to her father of all the children.

Charles took to Diana that weekend and began seeing her on a regular basis when they returned to London. She was only eighteen and still quite unsophisticated but, after all the glossy and sophisticated women he had gone out with, that was part of her appeal. She was fun and easy to be with, natural and down to earth, yet she was sensitive and courageous in the way she had coped with her father's illness. She had no expectations and made no demands. The Prince could relax, be himself and simply enjoy her friendship. He would ring her up every couple of months or so and invite her to the opera, or to dinner and no one paid any attention to this.

After Mountbatten's death, Diana's qualities were especially appealing. She was there with the warmth, sympathy and understanding that few others could offer. She instinctively knew what he was going through, drawing from the experience of her own troubled past; and he found himself growing increasingly fond of her.

The media, in the meantime, were clamouring for him to marry. It had been a preoccupation for several years, but now it was becoming intense. Even his father

With Prince Andrew and Charles at a polo match. What Diana craved was the security of marriage

had started badgering him. He had a duty, he was reminded, to secure the line of succession, to produce an heir to safeguard the monarchy. He was over thirty: it was no longer an intrusion into his privacy; it was rightly a matter of public concern. He must stop dallying with film stars and floozies and get on and find a wife.

Charles looked around for a suitable candidate and nudged, no doubt, by a couple of doting grandmothers, found Lady Diana Spencer. She was eminently suitable, well liked by everyone and was ready and waiting. What had begun as a schoolgirl crush had grown into a profound and romantic desire to be Charles's bride. She had no ambitions for a career. What she craved was the security of marriage and was only too pleased when Charles began to take her seriously during the summer of 1980. They saw a great deal of each other, but, because Diana was so much younger and usually just one of a party, no one who saw them together ever suspected she was a girlfriend. It was not until September when she was spotted with Charles on the banks of the River Dee at Balmoral by the royal reporter, James Whittaker, that anyone was any the wiser. At that point life changed more than anyone could have foreseen. The press laid siege to Diana's flat in London and followed her every move until the engagement was announced five months later.

They were testing months. Diana had no form of protection, and no help in dealing with the press. She had never been exposed to anything like it before, and initially she found being the centre of attention quite amusing. The sight of dozens of photographers leaping to their lenses every time she opened her front door made her giggle. She enjoyed giving them the slip, as she sometimes succeeded in doing. On one occasion she packed up her car as if about to go away for the weekend, then sauntered up the street, leading the press to believe she had gone to buy a packet of

March 1981, Diana's first official engagement. The press still followed her every step

Polos. By the time she reappeared, she had been up to Scotland and back, to spend the weekend with Charles at the Queen Mother's home, Birkhall.

She coped with the press with astonishing skill for someone who was just nineteen years old, and was always painstakingly polite. But as time went on, it became less of a joke. Journalists rang her day and night, even in the early hours of the morning. They kept up a twenty-four-hour vigil outside Coleherne Court, and plagued her at the kindergarten. They followed her wherever she went. Stories appeared that were untrue, newspapers quoted things she had not said and she began to feel panicky. Charles was worried she might be scared off. Her mother was so worried she wrote to *The Times* asking, 'Is it fair for any human being, regardless of circumstances, to be treated in this way?' In the House of Commons sixty MPs tabled a motion 'deploring the manner in which Lady Diana Spencer is treated by the media', and 'calling on those responsible to have more concern for individual privacy'. And the Press Council called senior editors to the first extraordinary meeting convened in its twenty-seven-year history to discuss the matter. Despite all this, nothing changed. The public's fascination with 'Shy Di', as she was dubbed, was simply insatiable.

In February the engagement was announced and Diana was rescued. She now came under the giant umbrella of the Royal Family and at last the palace was able to give her full protection. A personal bodyguard was assigned to her and has been with her day and night ever since. Gone were the last vestiges of normality. As she left Coleherne Court she left a poignant note for her flatmates, giving them her new telephone number: 'For God's sake ring me up – I'm going to need you.'

4

After the Honeymoon

Diana meant every word of her note. Friends have been of paramount importance to her in the last ten years and she has not deserted them. She may have become an international superstar, wined and dined with kings and presidents, prima ballerinas, film idols, pop legends and sporting heroes; she may be ferried around in motorcades and private yachts and planes; and she may be given priceless jewels to wear. Yet the people who truly matter in her life are the friends she had when she was an ordinary teenager. These are the people who have seen her through the difficult times, who have helped her adjust to the life before her and who have kept her in touch with the real world.

'Here is the stuff of which fairy tales are made,' proclaimed the Archbishop of Canterbury, Dr Robert Runcie, to a packed cathedral, on that famous wedding day.

'Here is the stuff of which fairy tales are made.' The wedding millions flocked to see

Back at Balmoral, Charles and Diana were classic newly-weds

Relaxed and happy aboard the Royal Yacht Britannia *at Gibraltar, at the start of their honeymoon in the sun*

Before him sat Queen Elizabeth II, the Queen Mother and every member of the British Royal Family; and most of the crowned heads of Europe, innumerable monarchs from Africa, the Middle East and Asia, including the 25-stone King of Tonga, for whom an extra-large chair had been specially made. There were 160 foreign presidents and prime ministers, dozens of high-ranking diplomats, civil servants, local government officials, members of the armed forces, politicians and industrialists.

Yet seated side by side near the front – ahead of Nancy Reagan, America's First Lady, and many other dignitaries – were those three girls from Coleherne Court: Ann Bolton, Virginia Pitman and Carolyn Pride. There were other friends too and people she had grown up with.

Not far behind them sat David Thomas and his wife, a jeweller who had looked after the Spencer family for years and sold Diana several pieces: but he was still 'just a humble jeweller', and was expecting to be tucked away behind a pillar at the back. This has to be a mistake, he had thought, as they were directed ever closer to the front. It was no mistake. Humble jeweller or not, as far as Diana was concerned he was a friend.

To their surprise, all the workers from Althorp were there too. They had been told by Earl Spencer that there were sadly insufficient tickets for him to invite them, but

Diana used her own allocation to ensure they were there. State occasion or not, it was her day and she wanted to be surrounded by her friends.

She may have been just twenty years old, and secretly terrified, but she would only have one wedding in her life, and she was determined to make it her own. And for all the pomp and ceremony, for all the formality and precision, the security and the months of planning, for all the cameras and lights, it was still a touching and surprisingly intimate affair.

The couple were determined their honeymoon should be too, despite equal determination on behalf of the world's press to keep them company. After a few days at Broadlands, they flew to Gibraltar to join the Royal Yacht *Britannia* for a two-week cruise in and around the Mediterranean. For two weeks the press flew from one Greek island to another, like migrating birds, at the slightest rumour. They set to sea in boats and cruisers; one newspaper even hired a Lear jet, which flew over the area day after day. But thanks to the ingenuity of Edward Adeane, who planned it all, no one found them.

It was the first and last time they have had such privacy and they returned to Balmoral to join the Royal Family for their traditional September break, tanned, relaxed and obviously very much in love. Within days of arriving they held a press

For two weeks they managed to evade the press. It was the first and last time they have ever had such privacy

conference, on the understanding that the press would thereafter leave them alone, and it was the most informal such occasion anyone can remember. They were classic newly-weds, unable to take their eyes or their hands off each other, laughing and joking and clearly very happy.

Their honeymoon had been 'fabulous', said Diana, bubbling over with enthusiasm and dying to tell the world. She could 'highly recommend marriage', she said. 'It's a marvellous life, and Balmoral is one of the best places in the world.'

The last year had been like a dream, a fairy tale; but suddenly, as the cameras retreated and the curtains drew on another quiet Balmoral evening, with the Queen insisting on formal dress for dinner, as she does every night, the dream began to dissolve. The honeymoon was over and the reality of what she had taken on began to dawn.

Diana had known she was marrying into a close family, but she was unprepared for how claustrophobic it would be, or how dull she would find long spells in their company, with their passion for dogs and horses. She had also known that Charles would have to see his mother just as regularly after they were married as before: there were matters of state they had to discuss, and discuss in private. It was part of the job: his mother was sovereign, he was her heir and they would share secrets that no one else could ever know. Rationally, Diana understood, but emotionally, the Queen was still her mother-in-law and the relationship was as difficult as for any new wife.

With the Queen at the Braemar Games. The honeymoon was over

Their weeks in Scotland were an anti-climax. Her husband, who had been so attentive in the sunshine, was back on home territory, in the place he loved best on earth, surrounded by the people and the activities he loved most. He was also back to the daily pile of paperwork and would be closeted with secretaries for much of the day. When that was done, he would be off fishing, thigh deep in the River Dee for hours on end, or shooting. Diana did not especially care for either of those activities and she did not ride, which kept the rest of the family amused. Not surprisingly, she grew bored and lonely. She longed for something to do other than trudge the glorious, heather-clad grouse moors. The weather did not help. It rained almost every day, and she began to feel imprisoned. She railed against the formality and the dreariness of it all, balked at the routine; her mood swinging back and forth, from tears and misery to elation. She wanted to go home, but it was out of the question. There was no alternative but to grin and bear it.

Returning to London was not the cure. Diana had been blaming the Highlands for what was a far more fundamental malady. Charles had been a bachelor for thirty-two years. He had a house in Gloucestershire and another at Kensington Palace, and staff who had been with him for years, accustomed to his simple and masculine lifestyle and accustomed to ruling it. He had a well-established routine in his life. He would rise early to work at his desk and return to it after a day's engagements, often until well past midnight. His sports and hobbies frequently took him away for the best part of the weekend; work also ate into parts of Saturday and Sunday. For the remainder of his free time, he had

Diana had never had any real discipline in her life. Charles had known nothing else

an established circle of good friends, whom he saw regularly. Most important of all, when duty called, Charles was there. Whether it was the Trooping of the Colour, a state visit, or Remembrance Sunday, whatever the time or day of the week, the dates were in his diary and he was on parade without fail and without question.

It never occurred to Charles that Diana would find any of this odd or difficult to accept; but her upbringing had been entirely different. She had never had any real discipline in her life in the way Charles had. She had done as she pleased. If she wanted to give up on something she did. She had never been pushed academically, although there is no doubt she had the intelligence to have done far better than she ever did. She had walked away from finishing school and she had walked away from Miss Vacani's; and her parents had never sought to interfere with her freedom, or impose restrictions on her.

Charles, by contrast, had known nothing but restriction and discipline. His life had been ruled by others from day one. He can never remember a time when he didn't have a detective to guard him, or private cars, planes or trains to transport him. He had never been able to lose himself in a crowd, or dash off somewhere suddenly on a whim. He had lived in castles and palaces, and been attended by courtiers, soldiers and valets.

Much as his parents might have wanted Charles to have a normal upbringing, it was impossible. They sent him to proper schools – the first royal child not to have been educated by private tutors – but he was never just another pupil; he was never allowed to forget the accident of birth that set him apart.

He grew up in the public spotlight, never free from prying eyes and press comment, never sure when a trusted friend would betray him, or when a casual remark to a stranger might blow up in his face. Sent away to prep school at eight, he was lonely and homesick and no sooner had he settled in than he moved to public school, to Gordonstoun, a bleak and desolate place on the windswept north-east coast of Scotland, with a regime to match. For the first three years he endured abject misery. At the point when he began to enjoy himself, he was sent off to go through it all again in Australia, in order that the Commonwealth could be seen to have played some part in his education. For six months he lived in even more spartan conditions at Timbertop, in the Australian bush. Again he had to prove himself, this time to 135 tough young teenagers aged fourteen and fifteen who were not impressed by his title.

It was a crash course in survival, and in learning how to get on with people; but when he made friends there, he knew, probably for the first time in his life, that he was liked for who he was and not what he was.

His three years at Cambridge were some of the happiest of his life and also the most normal. Apart from having a detective, who lodged in the room next door at Trinity, he lived like everyone else – except that yet again his course was interrupted. In the midst of his second year he was sent off to the University College of Wales at Aberystwyth, for a crash course in everything Welsh prior to his investiture as Prince of Wales in the summer of 1969.

It was not an easy transition. Prince Charles had a rough reception and a difficult, at times terrifying three months at the hands of extreme Welsh nationalists. Groups like the Welsh Language Society and the Free Wales Army were said to be training freedom fighters in the mountains and he was barracked everywhere he went.

A. J. P. Taylor called the decision to send Charles to Aberystwyth a 'sordid plot to exploit' him. 'Mr Wilson', he said, 'is imposing on Prince Charles a sacrifice which he would not dream of imposing on his own son.'

It was indeed a sacrifice and one from which many a twenty-year-old would have turned and run. So intense was the hatred in the town that, shortly before Charles was due to arrive, the principal of University College, Dr Tom Parry, had advised the visit be called off. Never before had the Prince encountered such anger and hostility, nor been exposed to such real and persistent danger. His mentor during the stay was the Secretary of State for Wales, George Thomas (later created Lord Tonypandy), who became a lifelong friend as a result. He knew that it was no use shielding Charles. He had to face the enemy.

Charles needed no pushing. One particular day, having struggled through an ugly crowd of protesters to the safety of the Welsh Office, the Prince announced he was going back out to talk to them.

'I would advise against it, sir,' said George Thomas.

'I know you would,' said Prince Charles, 'but I'm going.'

'In that case, sir,' said the Secretary of State, 'I'm coming with you.'

Sometimes it worked, sometimes they simply shouted abuse, but his greatest success was when he addressed the Welsh League of Youth Eisteddfod at Aberystwyth in Welsh, having studied the language for just six weeks. It was a hostile audience. The League had already declared that it would boycott the investiture and, when he stood up to speak, a hundred or so extremists began shouting and jeering, and dozens had to be dragged off by the police before he could be heard. Undaunted, he spoke for seven minutes to an audience of 5,000 people and won considerable respect from some hard-bitten nationalists, including Gwynfor Evans MP, president of Plaid Cymru. 'His performance was amazing,' he confessed, 'I have never heard anyone who has taken to Welsh so recently master the language so well.'

The investiture went ahead on 1 July and was a splendid and dramatic piece of pageantry; it was also strangely moving. As he knelt at his mother's feet, the sovereign invested her son with the symbols of office, 'by girding him with a Sword . . . by putting a Coronet on his head . . . and a Gold Ring on his finger . . . and also by delivering a Gold Rod into his hand, that he may preside there and may direct and defend those parts to hold to him and his heirs . . . for ever'.

'I, Charles, Prince of Wales,' responded the Prince, 'do become your liege man of life and limb and of earthly worship, and faith and truth I will bear unto you to live and die against all manner of folks.' With that, he took the letters-patent from his mother, rose to his feet, gave her the kiss of fealty, and took his place on the throne to her right.

A trade-union organizer from mid-Wales spoke for many an onlooker that day. 'I am not a royalist,' he said, 'I am a socialist and I wouldn't cross the street for the Prince myself. But I'll tell you this, that young man has done more for Wales already than we could dream of.'

At the age of twenty-two, the Prince's life was still being ruled by others. After university it was announced that he was going into the armed forces.

'It is pointless and ill informed to say that I am entering a profession trained in killing,' he said in his defence. 'The Services in the first place are there for fast, efficient and well-trained action in defence. Surely the Services must attract a large number of duty-conscious people? Otherwise, who else would subject themselves to being square-bashed, shouted at by petty officers, and made to do ghastly things in force ten gales? I am entering the RAF and then the Navy because I believe I can contribute something to this country by so doing. To me it is a worthwhile occupation and one which I am convinced will stand me in good stead for the rest of my life.'

These sort of sentiments had never crossed Diana's mind. In no way had she ever been prepared for the life she was now expected to lead and Charles had some difficulty in understanding her feelings. For all his altruism, he is intrinsically self-centred. Having been waited on hand and foot for most of his life and had people jump whenever he called, he has never really had the opportunity to be anything else. He had thought Diana would quietly fit into his routine.

Diana, for her part, thought she would become a wife and mother; but, with all the servants and secretaries who surrounded the Prince, including a valet who selected and prepared his clothes for the day, packed for him and even did his personal shopping, she felt superfluous, and just a little jealous. Some of them were loyal and trusted men who had been with the Prince for years and, as well as relying heavily upon them, he liked them. They enjoyed their position of confidence and some were a little resentful at having the boat rocked by the arrival of the Princess.

Some of the Prince's friends were also somewhat put out at having their cosy relationship altered by the distraction of a young wife. They had enjoyed his single status and the attention he devoted to them, and frankly did not want the intrusion of a newcomer. She, in turn, found some of his friends hard-going. She disliked the intimacy he showed towards some of them, was resentful of the memories they shared of which she was not a part, and felt excluded. She also found it intolerable to have her husband's old girlfriends around.

Apart from a handful of friends that were his own age, like Nicholas Soames and Lord Romsey – who were still fourteen or fifteen years Diana's senior – most of the people Charles enjoyed seeing were older, with the result that Diana frequently found she was socializing with her father's, or even grandfather's, generation. They were often men of learning, like Sir Laurens van der Post or the historian Sir Harold Acton. She was quite out of her depth and, frankly, bored.

Her own friends were poles apart from his. They were young, rich and ambitious, typical Hooray Henries, with Sloane Ranger girlfriends; Charles found them just as unsympathetic as they found him. It was no different from the situation that most couples face in the early days of their marriage, when they discover they don't like each other's friends. The way they dealt with it was no different from any other couple either, except that every move was being monitored by the media. Diana was accused of banishing the Prince's friends.

Learning the Job

D iana's first public engagement as Princess of Wales was, appropriately, a tour of the principality, and it was obvious from the very first day that she had an extraordinary talent. Whatever personal problems she and Charles had were put to one side and they gave the people of Wales a visit to remember. She plunged into the crowds, who had turned out in their thousands to greet her, as though she had been doing it all her life. She instinctively knew what to say to people and whose hand to clasp hold of.

'My dad says give us a kiss,' shouted a little boy at the first stop in Rhyl.

'Well then, you had better have one,' said Diana, and bent down to kiss him on the cheek.

She noticed one woman in the crowd was blind, and sought out her hand and squeezed it.

'What nice shiny medals,' she said, spotting a hunchbacked old soldier at the Deeside Leisure Centre. Then to his beaming wife, 'Did you polish them for him?'

And when the rain poured down in Carmarthen and the streets were like rivers, still the crowds stood out and waited. They were soaked right through to the skin and shivering in the cold. Diana looked half-frozen herself and battled with a useless umbrella; the feather on her hat began to flop, yet she stayed and chatted for longer than ever, as if to reward the people for their patience.

'Now I've seen her, she's everything I thought she would be,' said one woman. 'She's the flower in the royal forest.'

The Prince was bursting with pride, and amused to find himself redundant. At each stop they would take one side of the street each and he could not help notice the disappointment on people's faces if they got him rather than her. He was left apologizing for not having enough wives to go round.

'Do you want me to give those to her?' he would ask when people desperately pointed bunches of flowers in her direction. 'I seem to do nothing but collect flowers these days. I know my role.'

In three days they covered 400 miles. It was exhausting but exhilarating, not least of all because, in the middle of it, Diana learned that she was pregnant. It could not have been more exciting news and everyone was thrilled, but her small and newly

In Wales, the crowds turned out in their thousands to greet their new Princess, and they were not disappointed

gathered staff took a deep breath. They had only just recovered from dealing with all the correspondence and presents from the wedding; six days later, when the pregnancy became official, lorry loads of letters, bibs and baby boots rained down upon them.

Diana had gathered together a small staff who were learning the ropes as fast as she was. The principal members were a private secretary, Oliver Everett, who worked for the diplomatic service and was recalled from Madrid to set up her office; and Anne Beckwith-Smith, a specialist in eighteenth-century English painting, who worked at Sotheby's and was brought in as full-time lady-in-waiting. The task was to set up the office, get a system going to deal with the fan mail, gifts and general correspondence, liaise with dress designers and process the requests for patronages as they came in.

Within her first year Diana had been approached by 150 charities. She had chosen just five to start with, most of them to do with children, which seemed appropriate, and the Welsh National Opera, which was also fitting. Fond as she is of children, however, they are by no means her only interest. The Princess found herself pigeonholed for a long time as a result of those early associations, but they were nevertheless a useful apprenticeship.

Charles had his own household to deal with his affairs which he had brought together when he came out of the forces. David Checketts was his first private secretary, a former squadron leader in the RAF who had been equerry to the Duke of Edinburgh, and was the perfect person to help the Prince make the transition from the armed services into a full-time working member of the 'family firm'. He had left in 1979, when he felt he was no longer the right man for the job, and the Honorable Edward Adeane had replaced him. The man who ran the office was Michael Colborne, a chief petty officer whom Charles had become friendly with aboard HMS *Norfolk*, during his early days at sea. He was a trusted friend and one of the few people ever to have been in the Prince's employ who spoke frankly to him, and when asked would give an honest, if sometimes unwelcome, opinion.

Quite often Colborne would get an equally honest and unwelcome reply. The Prince has a fierce temper, which Colborne often caught the brunt of. On one occasion Lord Mountbatten had found him licking his wounds and asked if the Prince had been upsetting him.

'Bear with him, Michael, please,' said Mountbatten. 'He doesn't mean to get at you personally. It's just that he wants to let off steam, and you're the only person he can lose his temper with. It's a back-handed compliment really, you know. He needs you.'

It was Colborne as much as anyone who took Diana under his wing in the early days. They shared an office from the engagement to the wedding and he was a fatherly shoulder to cry on when the going was tough. Edward Adeane was not the man for the job. He was a brilliant lawyer, with a first-class brain, but very little tolerance of lesser intellects. He detested the commercial world and, although he was much the same age as the Prince, had no time for the young. He could no more understand what went on in a twenty-year-old's head than fly to the moon. When Diana once asked him what the capital of Australia was, he was rendered totally speechless.

Charles took on the job of improving Diana's geography and also of teaching her the tricks of the trade – how to handle the different sorts of engagements, how to remember names and avoid missing or offending anyone, how to pace herself, how to address people, what sort of questions to ask and how to steer clear of banana skins. Dealing with people came naturally and was in many ways the most important part of the job, but there was more that could come only with experience, and Charles was there to pass on some of the things he had learned over thirty-three years, some of them the hard way.

There was no job specification for the Prince of Wales and no guidelines for a Princess of Wales either. Their roles have just evolved. Charles had been moved early on by the plight of disadvantaged young people and much of his energy had gone into that. He had formed what later became the Prince's Trust while he was in the Navy, and the grants that went out in the early years were paid for, anonymously, out of his naval allowance. Candidates had to write down what they felt would most help them improve their lives and these suggestions were forwarded to the Prince in the diplomatic bag to wherever he happened to be in the world; he then chose whom the money should go to.

The scheme bore the unmistakable stamp of Kurt Hahn and his trust system that Charles had seen in operation at Gordonstoun. Applicants were given cash grants, usually no more than £75, and trusted to use it for the purpose they had proposed – such as buying a bicycle to do a newspaper round, obtaining equipment for a camping trip, or acquiring the wherewithal to learn a new skill or a sport. There was no bureaucracy, no strings: it was a straightforward gift. It would challenge young people's sense of responsibility, he hoped, and show these troubled teenagers that someone trusted and believed in them. It paid dividends and, as the scheme grew, many of the beneficiaries came back in order to help others.

As he went about the country talking to young people involved with the Trust, Charles could see at first-hand the tension that was building up in the vast depressing wastelands of the inner cities, where young people had no work, no ambition, no feeling of belonging, no pride in their surroundings – nothing, in fact, to get out of bed for in the mornings. In addition, there was racial tension.

During the Queen's Silver Jubilee Year in 1977 Charles had encountered a typical scene. He had been visiting a youth club in Lewisham, where twenty-four members, all black, had recently been arrested on mugging charges. As he arrived he was met by a rabble of noisy, angry youths. The one at the front, shouting loudest, was wearing a badge saying 'Stuff the Jubilee'. Charles walked straight up to him and asked what was wrong. When the boy told him how the police had made the arrests, the Prince called the division commander, whose men had arrested the twenty-four, to listen to what the boy had to say. Charles suggested they get together at a later date to sort it out.

This is precisely what happened. The twenty-four were tried by a court of law in the proper way, but the black community and the police began a dialogue that led to far better relations between the two than there had ever been before.

The Prince paid the price. He had been seriously out of line, he was told; meddling in dangerous and delicate situations where he had no business; going way beyond his brief. The criticism hurt, but it was from encounters like this that Charles discovered what his position as Prince of Wales was all about. It gave him, he realized, a unique ability. He could bring people together who would not under normal circumstances converse; and once they were talking, of course, there was hope.

The fearsome riots that swept the inner cities in 1981, in Brixton first, then Toxteth and Hansworth, Moss Side and Bristol, came as no surprise, and convinced Charles that this was the area where he could be of some use. Ignoring his advisers, he concentrated his efforts in finding ways of improving life for the young people living in those areas.

Diana had captivated the country; Charles was proud, but Diana was beginning to upstage him

Edward Adeane disapproved. Charles was taking the job a long way from the safe arena of charitable patronage and ribbon-cutting and into politically dangerous areas, where constitutionally, he ought not to be. Adeane was also unhappy about his association with Operation Raleigh, an ambitious round-the-world sailing venture, the second he had been involved with, run by the explorer John Blashford-Snell. The idea was to take young people from all sorts of backgrounds and countries, including the inner cities, and give them 'the challenges of war in peacetime': a combination of adventure and community service.

The Prince was becoming enthused, and as he grew more confident about the area he had targeted and took on more projects, he began to make increasingly serious and significant speeches.

At this point another problem reared its head. Diana had captivated the country and the obsession with her was showing no signs of abating. The media simply could not get enough. Whenever she accompanied him, whether to a glossy film première or a major speech, they reported on the clothes she was wearing, the hairstyle, the hat, the jewellery, whether she looked well, or strained or too thin. What Charles said in major speeches which he put a great deal of time and thought into, seldom went farther than the four walls he spoke within. The nation, it seemed, was far more concerned about the cut of Diana's coat than the crisis in society.

She started a craze for pearl chokers, which had not been seen in years. Culottes and ethnic jumpers, which she wore on her honeymoon, flooded the shops. And there was scarcely a shirt to be found that did not have the high necks and ruffles that she favoured in the early days. Women even cut their hair in the same style.

The Prince had had an inkling of what was to come in Wales, when the crowds had been so eager to see Diana that they could scarcely hide their disappointment if Charles and Diana took one side of the street each and they were on the side of the street he took. Then, he had been quite amused and content to joke about being nothing more than a flower bearer, but he was not so happy when it became a regular occurrence.

With the exception of his mother, he had never played second-fiddle to anyone. Every member of the Royal Family enjoys star status; they are used to being the centre of attention and there is strong unstated rivalry between them. In the normal course of events they will only be seen en masse after the Trooping of the Colour and on Christmas morning at Windsor; and the wisdom passed from experienced staff to newcomers is never to put them on stage together.

The situation became quite delicate. Proud though he was of his wife, Charles could not help noticing she was stealing the limelight. Even when he went to engagements on his own, people would ask why he had left her behind, where was she? For some reason, the public expected Diana to be with him wherever he went. Yet they never expected the Duke of Edinburgh to accompany the Queen everywhere, or Mark Phillips to be seen with Princess Anne.

The confidence he had gained from having a loving wife was being undermined by a feeling of rejection from the public. Subconsciously he was beginning to resent her; and there were flashes of anger when he accused his staff of paying her too much attention. The solution was to operate independently, to abide by the unwritten rules of royal management and not let the Prince and Princess get into a position where they were competing for the limelight except when the occasion was pure entertainment. But on 21 June 1982 the problem temporarily dissolved when at three minutes past nine in the evening, Diana gave birth to Prince William.

Parenthood

Having children so early in their marriage was a mixed blessing. Diana had felt unwell for much of the early part of her pregnancy, and was not quite herself, which made the process of settling down to married life all the more difficult. But William was a much loved and much longed-for baby, and the Prince and Princess could not have been happier.

Charles had taken an active interest from the start. He had wanted children for years: not having them had been the one drawback to marrying late. He had had to make do with friends' children, many of whom were his godchildren. He found them enormously relaxing to be with. Like animals, they are great levellers – not remotely impressed by a string of titles – and he always found he could build up a good rapport with them.

Having his own was his greatest wish and transformed his life. He went along to Diana's breathing classes to prepare for the birth and was there by her side in the private Lindo Wing at St Mary's Hospital in Paddington when William emerged after sixteen hours of labour. It was the most exciting, extraordinary experience he had ever had, and for a long time afterwards he would bend any ear he could find on the subject. Even at formal dinners where weighty matters were being bandied about, he would seek out other young fathers to swap stories with them about the thrill and magic of childbirth.

Both Charles and Diana were determined that their children were going to have normal, happy childhoods. They were convinced there should be no long periods of separation. Nannies were inevitable and, within their social set, also very much the norm; but the choice of Barbara Barnes to look after William was an indication that it was going to be a relaxed regime: she had no formal training, never wore uniform and liked children to call her by her Christian name. Most important of all, she had a healthy sense of humour. There was no way that any nanny in the Wales household was going to become a substitute for either parent. Charles became as adept at changing nappies and bathing William as Diana, and, even when he was small, both spent as much time as they could with him.

Thus when they flew up to Balmoral for the first time after his birth, the entire family travelled together, despite the merchants of doom who insisted they should

A protective Prince angrily telling photographers to leave his wife alone at a polo match

never fly together in the same plane lest it crash and kill both heir and second-in-line to the throne. On landing, it was Charles who carried the baby-basket off the plane and the nanny carried the bags.

When they set off the following year on a tour of Australia and New Zealand, William, as well as two nannies and acres of baggage, went too. Charles and Diana are both very fond of the Antipodes – Charles feels particularly at home there after his months at Timbertop – but it was a long and exhausting tour. They were away from home for six weeks and in that time covered thousands of miles, made over forty flights, attended a multitude of receptions, galas and banquets and shook more hands in walkabouts than could ever be counted. Once again, everyone wanted a glimpse of Diana, everyone wanted to touch her. Being able to return to William in the evenings brought back a sense of reality and made a difference to the whole trip.

Parenthood affected Charles dramatically. It focused his mind on the future and about the world that his small and fragile son would one day inherit. It made him re-evaluate his philosophy, his life, and gave him a whole new perspective. He entered, as he explained to me later, what Carl Jung would probably have described as 'the middle period'. The press interpreted it as encroaching lunacy.

It began with a speech to the British Medical Association. It was a glittering occasion, their 150th anniversary, and Charles was president. Agonizing over what to say, he was suddenly struck by inspiration. 'The most extraordinary thing happened,' he explained, 'I was sitting here [at his desk in Kensington Palace], and I happened to look at the bookshelf, and my eyes settled on a book about Paracelsus. So I took the book down and there was my speech; and the response to it was extraordinary. I've never had so many letters. I've been a great believer in intuition ever since.'

His speech dealt the BMA a devastating blow:

I have often thought that one of the less attractive traits of various professional bodies and institutions is the deeply ingrained suspicion and outright hostility which can exist towards anything unorthodox or unconventional.

Perhaps we just have to accept it is God's will that the unorthodox individual is

Leaving hospital with Prince William. Charles was thrilled to be with Diana at the birth

Becoming pregnant so early in their marriage was a mixed blessing. The Trooping of the Colour in June 1982

doomed to years of frustration, ridicule and failure in order to act out his role in the scheme of things, until his day arrives and mankind is ready to receive his message.

I would suggest that the whole imposing edifice of modern medicine, for all its breathtaking successes is, like the celebrated Tower of Pisa, slightly off-balance.

It is frightening how dependent upon drugs we are all becoming and how easy it is for doctors to prescribe them as the universal panacea for our ills.

Wonderful as many of them are, it should still be more widely stressed by doctors that the health of human beings is so often determined by their behaviour, their food and the nature of their environment.

The speech sent shock waves through the medical profession, but the Prince had hit a nerve and, for all the criticism that was heaped on his head in the aftermath, the letters from the public told him he had been right. Furthermore, it was spoken from the heart. Charles believes in the Platonic ideal of a healthy mind in a healthy body, plenty of exercise, self-help and positive thinking. He strongly believes that if there is a chance someone's suffering can be helped by an alternative method, then why not let them try it.

A year later another professional body, also celebrating its 150th anniversary, had its feet kicked from under it. Charles had long been interested in architecture – he had grown up with beautiful buildings and visited hundreds more all over the world; he had read extensively on the subject and, by the very nature of the job, had seen a multitude of buildings, especially in the inner cities, that not only looked ghastly, but that people clearly found ghastly to live in.

So, as the architects comfortably settled back into their chairs cradling their after-dinner brandies in preparation for some regal platitudes, the Prince launched into a stinging attack that left them reeling. It was time they stopped designing buildings without a thought for the people who had to live in them, he said. The proposed extension to the National Gallery looked like 'a kind of vast municipal fire station – complete with the sort of tower that contains the siren. I would better understand this type of "high-tech" approach if you demolished the whole of Trafalgar Square and started again with a single architect responsible for the entire layout. But what is proposed is like a monstrous carbuncle on the face of a much-loved and elegant friend.

'What have we done to our capital city? What have we done to it since the bombing of the last war?'

And of the proposed Mansion House Square project, he went on, 'It would be a tragedy if the character and skyline of our capital city were to be further ruined and St Paul's dwarfed by yet another giant glass stump better suited to downtown Chicago than to the City of London.'

Charles had savaged the soft underbelly of yet another hallowed institution and has not been forgiven to this day. Once again, however, he discovered he had struck a chord with ordinary people, people who had felt they were unfit to pass judgement on modern buildings because they lacked the qualifications. And although many architects still find it hard to say Charles's name without curling their lips, most of them do admit that by bringing the whole subject into the public domain, architecture has had a much-needed shot in the arm.

In 1984, however, they were admitting nothing. They were furious, as Charles had known they would be. He had not made the speech lightly, a considerable amount of thought and soul-searching had gone into it, and it was against the advice of most of his staff that he went ahead with it. Community architecture had come about as a reaction to the tower blocks of the 1960s which were clearly not working: they had led to vandalism and mugging and terrifying isolation for the people who lived in them. Charles had recently met a number of community

Arriving with Prince William in Alice Springs, Australia, at the beginning of a long tour in 1983

A touch of tenderness at Newcastle Stadium, New South Wales

architects and what they said, in the light of the depression he found in the inner
cities, made such perfect sense and was so inspirational that he felt compelled to
bring it to a wider audience.

There was one more group dealt a glancing blow by the Prince around the same
time: and this was Britain's farmers. Lawrence Woodward, director of Elm Farm
Research Centre, a small newly formed charity set up to research and develop·
organic agriculture, wrote to Prince Charles asking if he would speak at the first
organic food conference to be held in Cirencester in January 1983. Charles could
not, but sent a message instead; not the tame few words that Woodward had drafted
for him, but something much more forthright:

> For some years now modern farming has made tremendous demands on the finite
> sources of energy which exist on earth. Maximum production has been the slogan
> to which we have all adhered. In the last few years there has been an increasing
> realization that many modern production methods are not only very wasteful but
> probably also unnecessary . . .
>
> I am convinced that any steps that can be taken to explore methods of produc-
> tion which make better and more effective use of renewable resources are
> extremely important. Even if it may be some time before they are commercially

acceptable, pioneer work is essential if our planet is to feed the teeming millions of people who will live on it by the twenty-first century.

I shall be watching the practical results with interest to see what might be applicable to our work in the Duchy of Cornwall, for I am sure that there will be lessons that we can learn.

The conference had nothing like the coverage of either the British Medical Association or Royal Institute of British Architects festivities, so its impact on the public at the time was negligible; but it marked a significant turn in the Prince's own farming methods, brought environmental concerns slowly into consumer consciousness and in the long term dealt a devastating blow to the agrochemical industry.

The Duchy of Cornwall, where Charles had promised to apply the lessons of organic agriculture, is one of the largest estates in Britain, about 130,000 acres in all, of which the greater part is on Dartmoor. The remainder is farmland, mostly in the West Country, plus forty-five acres in south London, including the Oval cricket ground. The Prince inherited it upon becoming Prince of Wales and will lose it if and when he becomes King. In the meantime, it is his only source of income and he has to pay for everything out of it, both his personal and official expenses, including the upkeep of his and Diana's homes, their household, their wardrobes, the children's schooling, the official cars, and the cost of entertaining. He also pays 25% of that income to the Treasury in lieu of tax. Neither he nor Diana receives a penny from the Civil List. The only expense that is paid for is air transport, when they use aircraft of the Queen's Flight, the Royal Train, and the Royal Yacht *Britannia*.

The title Duke of Cornwall and the estate to go with it dates back to 1337, when Edward III created it to give his eldest son, the Black Prince, an income and somewhere to live; it was he who decreed that it should always go to the eldest son. So if there is no son, as during George VI's reign, it is held by the monarch.

When Charles came of age in 1969, the Duchy had been in abeyance for thirty-three years and was seriously rundown; much of it was yielding nothing. Although administered by a council, which met three times a year to review policy, it had undergone none of the post-war modernization and investment that had rescued the rest of the farming industry from the crippling effects of war. No one seemed to have realized that Charles would need an income when he came of age. Land stewards had become autonomous, farm buildings had fallen into disuse, land had been poorly managed, properties had been allowed to run down and rents had gone unreviewed.

If the Prince was going to be able to live off it when he finished his naval career and support the wife that everyone seemed so desperate for him to acquire, something radical had to be done. So in 1972 a new secretary was appointed for the task, Anthony Gray, who worked away for some years and helped set it on its feet again. Once he came out of the Navy, Charles became a little more involved, but it was not really until the end of the decade, after Mountbatten's death, when he was looking for a real job to do, that Charles took up the reins himself. In so doing he found another character, John Higgs, who became central to his development. Charles and John Higgs clicked, and it was largely thanks to the relationship struck up with him, and the sheer personality of the man, that Charles became wholly and genuinely enthused by every aspect of the Duchy.

Charles had said he wanted a practical farmer on the council who knew something about estate management, and John Higgs was the man found for the job. He had been the estate bursar at Oxford, and there was little about farming, estate management, rural development and conservation that John Higgs did not know. He was a grey-haired dynamo of a man, bursting with ideas and good humour, who was not afraid to speak his mind to the Prince of Wales. When Tony Gray retired in 1981, Higgs became secretary.

Charles had known next to nothing about farming. The Queen has a large farm at Windsor, which the Duke of Edinburgh manages, and another at Sandringham; and she herself is very knowledgeable about livestock and pedigrees, as is the Queen Mother. But Charles knew very little and nothing at all about management, business and finance. His education had not prepared him for this in any way.

John Higgs gave him a crash course. He inspired the Prince, worked alongside him, coached him in the ways of business, schooled him in the art of responsible land management, encouraged him to try out new ideas, and helped turn the Duchy from a non-profit-making concern into one that five years later had made net profits of £1.46 million.

With a wife and child to support Charles needed to make the Duchy profitable. The family in Auckland, New Zealand, in 1983

Highgrove

aving set the Duchy on the road to providing an income for the Prince of Wales, the next task had been to find him a house and, of all those short-listed in the summer of 1980, Charles chose Highgrove.

He had specifically wanted somewhere with a farm and Highgrove had 410 acres; also, to be within easy range of his friends and relatives, and again it fitted the bill. It was a few miles outside the pretty market town of Tetbury in Gloucestershire; two hours from London down the M4 motorway, with easy access to Wales and the West Country; close to Princess Anne's house, Gatcombe Park; his friends, the Parker-Bowles; and not far from Windsor. It was also not far from Cirencester Park, Cowdray Park and Smith's Lawn for polo. What is more, it was in the midst of Beaufort Hunt country and the Prince was hunting two or three times a week during the season.

What it was not, however, was either very large or very grand. It had been previously owned by Maurice Macmillan MP, son of the late Conservative Prime Minister Lord Stockton, and the Duchy paid over three-quarters of a million pounds for the property. From the security point of view it was uncomfortably close to the road, and had a public footpath (which has since been re-routed) running across the garden, no more than two or three hundred yards from the house, but the Prince liked it. He especially liked the old and rare trees that had been planted in the garden by a previous owner, Colonel Mitchell, who bought the house in 1893. He was a great expert, founder of the arboretum at Westonbirt nearby, and he filled every vista with a dazzling display of ornamental and specimen trees, which the Prince has since added to.

Owning a home of his own was a huge pleasure, but greater still was the pleasure of having a garden of his own. All the royal residences have magnificent gardens and he had grown up appreciating them, but they are tended by gardeners: neither the Queen nor the Duke of Edinburgh is interested. The gardener of the family is the Queen Mother, whose gardens at her Scottish hideaways, the Castle of Mey and Birkhall, are stunning, and it is she who over the years has made them so.

So Charles had the will but not the way and called on his friend Lady Salisbury to help. Mollie Salisbury had designed several gardens for friends, as well as her own at

Hatfield House in Hertfordshire, and she was only too delighted to help plan a garden from scratch. When Charles moved in to Highgrove there was practically no garden at all, just acres of lawn and some box hedges. There was also a walled kitchen garden, which had been let go to grass, and a large hole had been knocked into one of the walls to let the tractor in to mow it.

With Mollie Salisbury's help, Charles designed his entire garden, and furthermore, with the assistance of just one gardener, he dug it, manured it and planted it too. He discovered in the weeks and months that passed a real passion; a task that was not only deeply therapeutic, but one that he also found he could do rather well. Lady Salisbury describes him as 'a natural plantsman'.

What Charles also wanted now he had a garden of his own was wild flowers. The greatest wild-flower expert in this country is Dr Miriam Rothschild, who had known Charles since he was a child, and was also a friend of Mollie Salisbury. She ran the Royal Society for Nature Conservation, founded by her father in 1912, of which the Prince is patron. In conjunction with her passion for insects and butterflies, on which she is a leading authority, she had a scheme underway to reintroduce wild flowers to the countryside. She still travels the world, tirelessly delivering papers at scientific gatherings and converting anyone she comes across on the way. Charles was one such, and he invited her to Highgrove to work her magic.

She is no romantic. Although she enjoys the aesthetic value of wild flowers, her reason for encouraging their widespread growth is principally scientific. A vast range of plants are used in medical preparations and as research continues new species are found to have beneficial properties. If a species is allowed to become extinct, however insignificant it may have appeared to be, that is one potential medication lost to mankind for ever.

At that time it was the idea of looking out over fields of swaying poppies and corn-flowers that appealed to the Prince. On a strip of land between the house and the kitchen garden over ninety species of wild flower now grow. More grow alongside the drive and are a lasting pleasure to him.

The garden was and still is his paradise and his pride and joy, and whenever Charles has the time he will put on a pair of old trousers, find a spade and get down to some real manual labour. He now has two gardeners working full time: Dennis, a grand old boy who has scarcely been out of Gloucestershire in his life – and has been looking after foxhounds for the Duke of Beaufort for most of it; and Trevor Jacobs, a younger and professionally qualified horticulturist.

Dennis presides over the walled garden, which supplies the kitchens at Highgrove and Kensington Palace and grows all the weird and wonderful varieties that the Prince acquires and delights in surprising his guests with. He had ten varieties of carrot in the ground when I visited, including a purple carrot that has not been grown since the eighteenth century. The entire garden is organic; and any new idea that the Prince picks up in his travels, he immediately tries out at home. The walled garden is divided by stone-chip paths with neat low box hedges, and there are flowers and

William and Harry have a tree house to play in in the woods at Highgrove

In the gardens of Kensington Palace; but Charles was happiest in the gardens of Highgrove

herbs growing alongside the vegetables. In the middle there is a little pond with a fountain, and the golden carp that swim in it are so tame that they come at the sound of Dennis's voice. Dennis also looks after the fruit cage and the greenhouse, where he grows scented plants for the house, like stephanotis and jasmine. He works from dawn to dusk and then, for recreation, goes home to his little cottage in the grounds and tends his own little garden, growing prize specimens for the local show.

Trevor takes care of the rest of the garden, plants up the giant tubs that sit outside the house, helps the Prince plan new features and site new trees and additional flower beds. He also weeds the existing beds, prunes the roses and, as well as all the other seasonal jobs, cuts the lawns and hedges. There are dozens of hedges, which the Prince is growing in order to create topiary; there is also an avenue of trimmed and rounded golden yew trees leading the eye, in classic style, to a folly at the foot of the park.

It is an exciting garden, the hedges and paths divide it so that you come upon different parts almost by surprise, such as the scented garden, the woodland garden, built around some of the trees that Colonel Mitchell left behind him, with a sturdy wooden tree-house for the children, and the patio garden where the Prince sits and does paperwork during the summer months to the soothing sound of water, which springs from a sculpture he commissioned of stone whales.

The folly was a gift from the Sultan of Oman, just one of the many presents that now adorn the property. The giant wrought-iron entrance gates, for example, came from the people of Tetbury, the fruit trees espaliered against the walls of the vegetable garden were presented by the Worshipful Company of Fruiterers and the herbs came from a women's institute in Sussex. The small heated swimming pool hidden from view near the rose walk was a wedding gift from the Army.

The whole estate is a reflection of the Prince's philosophy about the countryside. He has built a new cowshed in the last year, and it is of brick and Cotswold stone – in keeping with the existing buildings. The dry-stone walls have been repaired in the traditional way; fences in the fields to keep the animals back are wooden post-and-rail, there is no barbed-wire to be seen; and where the Prince has planted new trees in the parkland, they are all protected from the livestock by solid wooden guards, not the plastic sort most farmers use. Sheep graze within view of the house and also a herd of Aberdeen Angus, and a number of horses, some with foals. To complete the idyllic farmyard scene, chickens, a mixture of varieties, strut and scratch about the driveway and the fields.

Charles was keen to use his estate at Highgrove as an example for the rest of the Duchy. In bringing it up to date and making it profitable, he had to tread warily, for although it was made up of land and property, it was essentially about people. Rents needed to be brought up to a realistic level, housing stock modernized, particularly in some of the rundown areas of Kennington, and surplus sold off, without souring relations with his tenants. So he began to involve them in some of the decision-making about how their environment might be improved, their needs met. He called meetings to solicit their views and thus began his own experiments with what was effectively community architecture.

On the rural side he had 180 tenant farmers, each with between 50 and 130 acres apiece; and just as the Prince wanted the goodwill of his urban tenants, so too in the country. So he and John Higgs made frequent forays into the countryside giving farmers no more than twelve hours' notice of the intended visit. Higgs insisted on this so their wives would not be caught in curlers; but the idea was that Charles should see the farms and the farmers as they really were, not spruced up and on parade. Charles wanted the farmers to talk frankly to him so he could learn about their lives and problems, and put what he learnt to good effect.

A frank talk was a help, but it was no substitute for knowing what it was like to have to milk cows at the crack of dawn every morning or mend fences, or battle with the elements, and so he began a series of annual stays on Duchy farms. He spent a week working alongside the farmer, mucking out cattle yards, feeding pigs, dipping sheep; and living as a guest in his house. Charles thoroughly enjoyed the experience and it was a rare opportunity to see how ordinary people lived. The media, once again, saw it as further indication of encroaching madness.

The Prince feels he has a responsibility as a landowner to set an example to others, always to take the humane or the conservationist route above the straight commercial. Early on, working in tandem with John Higgs, he had brought in the Farming and Wildlife Advisory Group and the Nature Conservancy Council to look at all the farms on the estate to make sure they were farming with conservation in mind. His preoccupation with conservation has grown over the years, but even then it was nothing new. It was a subject Charles had been actively concerned about for most of his adult life. It had even been the topic of his first public speech in 1968.

He had grown up with a love of the countryside. The Royal Family are country people, their interests and off-duty activities are all to do with the countryside, and the Prince always had a good knowledge of its workings; but it was not until after he became chairman of the steering committee for Wales that he discovered the danger it was in.

He said:

We are faced at the moment with the horrifying effects of pollution in all its cancerous forms. There is the growing menace of oil pollution at sea, which almost destroys beaches and certainly destroys tens of thousands of seabirds. There is chemical pollution discharged into rivers from factories and chemical plants, which clogs up the rivers with toxic substances and adds to the filth in the seas. There is air pollution from smoke and fumes discharged by factories and from gases pumped out by endless cars and aeroplanes.

Waste is yet another problem. When you think that each person produces roughly 21 lbs of rubbish per day and there are 55 million of us on this island using non-returnable bottles and indestructible plastic containers, it is not difficult to imagine the mountains of refuse that we shall have to deal with somehow.

The speech might have been delivered last week. In fact, it was twenty-one years ago, in February 1970. Even more prophetic words were to follow:

The list is longer, but what I am getting at is that it is going to be extremely expensive to cut down this pollution. In the end it will be the general public, as consumers, who will have to pay. Are we all prepared to accept these price increases for the sometimes dubious advantage of seeing our environment improved? Are we prepared to discipline ourselves to restrictions and regulations that we feel we ought to impose for our own good? If we are not, then this meeting and the whole of Conservation Year will have been a gigantic, costly and splendid waste of time.

Twenty-one years ago there were very few people who shared the Prince's point of view. Those who did were mostly long-haired, bearded and dressed in open-toed sandals. Even in the early 1980s, the press saw his adherence to the theme as one more idea to mock.

Charles, however, was determined to use the farm at Highgrove as a model to put his ideas into practice. After delivering his message of support to the organic movement at Cirencester, he held a seminar at Kensington Palace to air the issues, and he and John Higgs subsequently went down to Elm Farm to investigate the possibilities of employing organic methods on the home farm. The basic philosophy involves farming as far as possible within a closed system: in a nutshell, growing crops to feed the animals and using the manure those animals produce to fertilize the soil in order to grow more crops. The use of soluble chemical fertilizers is banned, as are hormone stimulants. The animals must be reared in humane conditions, which means that intensive operations – like battery henhouses or veal units – are forbidden.

Modern farmers now endeavour to dominate nature by using chemicals that ensure growth. The organic farmer works *with* nature, recognizing the intricate and holistic properties of agriculture, so that growth is encouraged and problems averted not by introducing an outside agent, but by structuring and adapting the system.

This philosophy appealed to Prince Charles and he was keen to give it a go, but, like everything else in the Duchy, the home farm had to pay its way. John Higgs had reservations. He felt a lot of hot air was talked by some of the purists. Nevertheless, he agreed to visit West

The Prince has always had a good knowledge of livestock

Germany on the Prince's behalf, where the movement was far more advanced, and report back. He returned after a very jolly trip, with a ten-pound carrot and a giant pumpkin, which he sent to Prince Charles. 'We found as much wind in Germany,' said the memo attached, 'as there is in this pumpkin.'

Wind notwithstanding, Charles decided to go ahead and experiment, initially on an eighty-acre block of land at Highgrove; this has proved so successful that, by the end of 1991, all the arable land on the farm will be up to organic farming standards.

John Higgs, alas, did not live to see it. He died after a very short and sudden illness in June 1986. Charles was shocked. He had lost another close companion, another friend, one who had helped and guided him and given him such pleasure. Before his death the Prince knighted John Higgs, and went specially to St Thomas's Hospital to perform the investiture at his bedside.

The Charitable Princess

A myth abounds that women just need to be told they are going to meet the Princess of Wales and they go into labour. It no doubt helps if they are already pregnant; but the notion is not as fanciful as it sounds.

In July 1984 the Princess had agreed to become patron of a small medical research charity called Birthright, which had been set up initially to try and minimize the dangers of pregnancy and childbirth. Diana's first visit in her new role was to open a new research centre at King's College Hospital, which dealt with the problems of high-risk babies; this had been funded by Birthright. It was the first centre of its kind, and was offering treatment to women who had suffered problems with previous pregnancies – women who had had handicapped babies, for example, or stillbirths.

The Princess had said she particularly wanted to meet mothers who had had a treatment known as chorionic villus biopsy, which was a very exciting break-through. It is a means of discovering at just eight weeks of pregnancy whether the foetus is normal. Birthright had funded its development in Britain, and this was its introduction at King's College Hospital. The charity's national organizer, Vivienne Parry, set about finding some mothers-to-be to meet the Princess; but as fast as she found them, they went into labour. This happened with no less than eight. On the morning of the visit, her final hope, a woman whose baby was due the following day, rang Vivienne to say she was getting pains. 'Well, cross your legs,' said Vivienne, now desperate, 'and get down here right away.' The woman did as she was told, met the Princess, and went into labour in the car on the way home.

This mother was a perfect example for the Princess to meet. Her first baby had been born with a genetic disease and had died, but the disease had not been diagnosed until she was pregnant with her second child. Fortunately, it was born healthy. When she became pregnant for the third time she was given an amniocentesis, the only form of testing available at that time. It meant she didn't know whether the foetus carried the disease until she was twenty-one weeks pregnant, by which time abortion is very difficult both physically and emotionally. The new treatment had meant that this woman was able to establish that her fourth baby was healthy when she was only ten weeks and two days into her pregnancy.

September 1985. Childbirth was no less magical the second time around with Prince Harry

It was a triumph of modern science, and the new patron could not have been more impressed – although being seven months pregnant herself she was a little bit squeamish at the sight of the giant ten-inch needles used in the procedure.

Whether Diana's interest in Birthright was planted by her obstetrician George Pinker, who was then its president, or by several of her friends who have had problems and become involved, her decision to add Birthright to her list of patronages marked a turning point in its history. In 1984 Birthright had an income of £600,000, and very few people had heard of it. The research it funded all took place in laboratories inside hospitals and there was nothing tangible to show for it. Diana opened the first research centre that treated patients. She went on to open more and more all over the country. She met 'miracle' babies and, at the less glamorous end of the scale, opened a cervical-cancer unit. In fact, it was the extra revenue she brought in at the baby end that enabled the charity to open up units for cervical cancer, and fund other research into unappealing but equally vital conditions. Through her involvement, Birthright has leapt from being a fringe charity into a major one. Its income is now £1,500,000 a year and rising fast.

Nothing could give the Princess more satisfaction. Her preference is for small charities where she feels she can do some good, and where she has some natural interest. The British Deaf Association (BDA) was another such charity. This had

The Princess has a curious effect on pregnant women. Diana visiting the Birthright unit at St Mary's Hospital, London

Diana immediately wanted to learn sign language after her first visit to a school for the deaf

been one of the 150 organizations that had written asking for patronage when Diana became engaged, and had been turned down. Then, quite out of the blue at the end of 1983, they had a letter from the Palace saying that the Princess had decided she would like to be their patron. It was no coincidence, perhaps, that its president was the Marquess of Salisbury, married to Mollie Salisbury who had spent so much time helping with the garden at Highgrove.

So Diana was among friends, but she was still enormously nervous on her first visit to the BDA headquarters in Carlisle. This was the beginning of her determination to learn sign language, which has been more of a boost to the deaf community over the years than any other gesture. Liz Scott-Gibson, who is now director of sign language services for the BDA, subsequently went to Kensington Palace to teach the Princess; and on a later visit, to a school in Durham, Diana surprised everyone by being able to communicate to the deaf people she met without an interpreter. Ever since, she has been delighting deaf people she encounters by communicating in their own language.

Dr Barnardo's was another charity she took on at about the same time; this charity has left its old orphanage image behind, and the Princess feels her connections with it have been fruitful. As with all her involvements, though, it was a gradual process. Diana was still the new girl in those days, very much learning as she went along, shy and unsure of herself, and leaning heavily on others for support and guidance. But Diana's impact on fund-raising was evident from the start. She only had to shake a hand to increase the revenue and bring more publicity to the organization than any amount of money could buy. Her presence was enough to make front-page news.

This was also true, of course, of the Prince. He may not have attracted the cameras in quite the way the Princess did, but he certainly brought recognition and respectability to every company or organization whose threshold he crossed. The prestige they reaped from a visit was incalculable. This was one aspect of his life that Charles found hard to come to terms with, especially during this period when he was evaluating and reassessing his role in life. For someone with his intellect, his was an intensely frustrating position. He was famous, people flocked to catch a glimpse of him, they stood for hours in the freezing cold in the hope that he would choose their hand to shake – for no better reason than an accident of birth. Charles constantly felt he had done nothing to earn it; there was no feeling of satisfaction in a job well done. He had not won an election, sung an aria, or even built up a business empire. He was famous simply because he happened to be the Prince of Wales; and in his darker moments he felt that charities and organizations only wanted him because of his name. The most useful contribution he could make was to turn up on the right day in the right uniform, cut ribbons, and make cosy speeches. When he did try to make some real contribution to society, it seemed that all he got for his trouble was criticism.

The Prince was too sensitive, too intelligent, to play the part mapped out for him, the part that his courtiers were there to help maintain. He longed to do some real work that would give him some satisfaction at the end of a day, yet there seemed to be nothing for him to do. He began to question the ethics of his whole position. His was one of the richest families in the world. He knew nothing but privilege. He lived in beautiful houses, travelled the world in the greatest of comfort, and wanted for nothing. This is how monarchs and their families have lived for generations, without ever questioning that it should be so. Charles was undergoing serious doubt.

His Prince's Trust brought him into contact with the real world. He repeatedly met people whose lives were desperate. Their living conditions were grim, their education was minimal, and their prospects for the future were bleak. It was not just the inner cities. There were no jobs for young people in rural areas; rising property prices meant that they were unable to find housing in the villages in which they had grown up. The problems did not stop there. During 1981 the Prince had been patron of the International Year of Disabled People, and met yet another vast group of people who suffered enormous hardship and prejudice, and whom society did not seem to care about. While grain mountains grew in the West, millions of people in the Sudan were dying of starvation. Practically nothing had been done for the environment since 1970; people had simply built more cars, more roads, more factories, and thrown ever-increasing tons of chemicals on to the land. It had turned out to be exactly as Charles had forecast, 'a gigantic, costly and splendid waste of time'.

There was so much to do; there were people out there whom the system was failing; there was a world that was being poisoned. But what could he do about it? He felt impotent, uncertain about what he should be doing, what was expected of him. With the exception of Michael Colborne, everyone within the Palace was telling Charles that he should not be getting involved. Adeane had strongly advised against the controversial speeches of the past year, especially the one to the architectural profession. He disapproved of the Prince's involvement in Operation Raleigh; he even felt that Charles's youth and inner-city work was politically border-line and unwise. Adeane counselled against it all, and was backed by the Duke of Edinburgh. Colborne was pulling the other way: he said there was a social revolution going on outside the Palace gates; he believed young people needed leadership as they never had needed it before, and the Prince was the one who could lead them.

Uncertain which route to take, and lacking the confidence to follow his instincts, the Prince turned in on himself. He retreated to Highgrove and took out some of his frustration on the soil and the polo field. At other times he revelled in the distraction of his children.

'Have a good weekend, sir,' said Harold Haywood, secretary of the Prince's Trust, one Friday night.

'Well, I was hoping to do some digging,' said the Prince, 'but it's so hard that I can't get the spade in. So I expect I'll be nappy changing instead.' Nappy changing it was, his detective confirmed, while the nanny had the weekend off.

There was a new baby in the house by this time. On 15 September 1984 Charles was once again by Diana's side at St Mary's Hospital when Prince Harry came into the world. The magic was every bit as exciting the second time around as it had been with William. Charles was fiercely proud of his wife and son, and felt that if there was any point to life at all, this was it.

This was another bone of contention with Adeane. As a bachelor, Adeane had no concept of the intense pleasure fatherhood had brought the Prince, and no understanding of why he should want to spend so much time at home. It seemed that when the Prince was not at home, he was playing polo. Adeane's function as private secretary appeared to be little more than the job of arranging the Prince's schedule around polo and the children's bath times.

The press had noticed too. They had calculated that in one particular three-month period Charles had had fifteen engagements, Princess Anne had carried out fifty-six, Prince Philip, forty-five, and the Queen, twenty-eight. The tabloids were calling Charles work-shy and lazy, and the Duke of Edinburgh told him to pull his socks up.

Colborne conceded that he was fighting a losing battle; a battle against the entire social structure within the Palace and the snobbery and jealousy of the Old Guard that surrounded the Prince. Colborne's departure was a shock to Charles. He was the one person within his household who had told him the truth; he had been his eyes and ears in the community, voiced the opinions of the man in the street. At times he had been his conscience too – when the Prince had lost his temper or been rude to someone, Colborne would write him a note and tell him so. He was devoted to the Prince, but he had served him for ten years and his wife had scarcely seen him. He was now fifty, and he felt she deserved more from her marriage. He left just a few days before Christmas in 1984.

Less of a surprise was Edward Adeane's departure the very next day. Charles summoned Adeane, they had yet another blazing row, and Adeane returned to the more predictable workings of the Bar. He had been an excellent courtier of the very best tradition. His misfortune was that Charles was not a traditional Prince of Wales.

It was not only his staff who found Charles difficult during this period. He is a man whose emotions are close to the surface, and who plunges into profound troughs. Although the arrival of Harry was a break in the gloom, the Prince was a prickly man to live with. He was tortured and temperamental and hugely demanding of everyone around him. Diana was sympathetic, but did not fully understand his unrest, nor his frantic soul-searching. She was twenty-three and simply too young to comprehend the feelings of middle age – let alone those of a middle-aged *prince*. Besides, she was very wrapped up in a world of her own. She had two delicious babies, she was a Princess, a star, and the world was her oyster. She was having a ball.

Admittedly, there were times for her when it all became too much, when the intrusion and the invasion were a strain. But there was a flip side to the coin. When she was dressed and made up and prepared for it, she enjoyed the attention, she enjoyed being photographed, and she found the sight of her face on the covers of magazines and newspapers enormously exciting. She loved wearing beautiful clothes and price-

Diana loves dressing up, wearing priceless jewels, and going to film premières

less jewels, and was thrilled to meet her favourite pop stars and actors, go to rock concerts, ballets, operas and glittering film premières. It was exciting to travel by private plane and helicopter with courtiers standing to attention, to be driven in a limousine the size of a small house, and to stay in palaces and castles in the lap of luxury. It was a far cry from life at Coleherne Court, where there was no one but herself to do the washing, ironing and vacuuming. Sometimes she had to pinch herself to make sure it was not all a dream.

Diana had been very young when she married Charles, and not just in years. She had seen none of this glamorous life; she had seldom even been to smart restaurants, let alone banquets and star-studded receptions. Despite her wealth and connections, her life had been quietly sheltered. She knew nothing of the drugs or drop-out culture of her generation. She dressed in clothes that her mother bought her, such as tartan skirts and matching jumpers, and seldom wore make-up. Hardly a head would turn if she walked into a room. She watched television, listened to music, and dreamed about favourite pop stars – just like any normal teenager.

In the first four years of her marriage that life had been turned on its head, transformed out of all recognition. She was famous the world over, in a way that no member of the Royal Family, not even any Hollywood legend, had ever been. People flocked in their thousands to see her, they hung on her every word, watched her every move on television.

In the same space of time she had married, embarked on a new and totally alien job, had a baby, celebrated her twenty-first birthday, and then had a second child – all momentous events in anyone's life, without the other pressures she was having to cope with. They had

Charles played polo unremittingly three or four times a week. Diana found his obsession hard to understand

been very heady years. Much as she might have wanted to help, Diana was in no position to give Charles the attention he needed.

In many respects she found him an enigma. She understood his need for sport, because she too enjoyed exercise; what she did not understand was his need to punish himself with such dangerous activities. In the summer months it was polo, which he played unremittingly three or four times a week. In winter he put his polo ponies out to grass at Highgrove, and got his hunters into peak condition. Again, three or four times a week he would push himself to the limit, galloping across the countryside with the hounds, risking life and limb in another of the most physically exacting sports known to man.

At other times he craved solitude and took himself off to Balmoral to fish, paint and stalk deer. Diana found his obsessions puzzling, and not a little hurtful. She could not understand why he should want to spend so much time away from home and his family.

9

Differing Interests

The Prince's behaviour was no reflection on Diana or their children. In those difficult months and years Charles was unaware of anyone but himself. He had reached a crossroads in his life. He had lost many of the people who mattered to him, and he was unsure of himself and his abilities. He knew he had a duty, but a duty to do what? To open buildings and preserve the royal status quo? Or to try and improve the lives of the people who would one day be his subjects?

Diana had married no ordinary man. Charles had never been carefree, never been allowed to be childish or make mistakes like his peers, never had friends to call on and pour his heart out to. His had been an isolated and lonely existence, despite the people perpetually at his side. He would never be able to settle down to married life like a suburban husband. He was a man apart, a man desperate to be of some use, driven to understand the purpose of life and his role within it.

Charles enjoyed the time he spent with his wife and children, but the events of the last four years had been no less momentous for him, and his way of coping with the stress and tensions in his life had always been by testing himself physically. He is not a natural extrovert; leadership was thrust on him from a very early age. The trials of his childhood and teenage years turned him into the perfect Prince, but they did not alter his fundamental nature. Public speaking is something he enjoys today, but it was a gruelling experience in the early days, as were walkabouts. City life, even in the environs of Kensington Palace, is a trial to the Prince; he feels suffocated by London and longs to escape to the country and be at one with nature.

Polo is the Prince's game because it was his father's game and also Mountbatten's; and it is the ultimate test. 'I am one of those people', he has said in the past, 'who must take exercise not only to be able to give of my best, but just to survive – I mean, I can't function without it. If I can have a game of polo I feel five hundred times better in my mental outlook. But without some form of exercise I'm afraid to say I get terribly jaded and – well, not depressed, but below par.'

Polo requires tremendous fitness, and 100 per cent concentration. It is a dangerous game, as he discovered yet again in the summer of 1990. But the Prince has always enjoyed flirting with danger, like his cousin, Prince William of Gloucester, who was killed in a plane crash in 1972. Charles had pushed himself to the limit in the armed

For the Prince it was the beginning of a love affair. In a gondola in Venice, April 1985

Charles would never be able to settle down to married life like a suburban husband. On the Royal Yacht Britannia *in 1985*

forces and had insisted upon doing the full training that his fellow officers did – despite protests from his superiors. He had done the Royal Marines commando training, he had insisted on parachute jumping and escaping from a tank in 100 feet of water in a simulated exercise – an exercise that killed two men over the next two years. Sometimes his superiors did put their foot down. There were a few exercises they forbade, and would never let the Prince pilot supersonic Buccaneers or the Sea King anti-submarine helicopters; but he did qualify for membership of the exclusive Ten Ton Club, by flying at more than 1,000 m.p.h. in a Phantom scrambled from Leuchars in Fife, which he had taken over Balmoral before going supersonic off the coast of Scotland. Unknown to most people, he had also driven a Formula Two racing car belonging to world-champion racing driver Graham Hill around the track at Thruxton – *and* come perilously close to disaster. He had lost control on the wet surface and spun right off the track.

But these were the things that made life worth living. Charles hated the feeling that he was being wrapped in cotton wool; he felt cheated when he was not allowed to do what other men did. If he could confront physical danger and win he could go to bed feeling that he had achieved something with his day. Horse riding was his route to this feeling. It was 'the sport of kings' after all, and however dangerous, Charles was determined that no one was going to take that pleasure away from him.

His other necessity in life was solitude. He had needed it ever since he was a child. Even as a schoolboy he had taken himself away from the crowd for long lonely walks, and sat in the silence of the small chapel in the grounds at Gordonstoun. Of all the community services on offer, he had chosen the coastguards, which involved nights spent quietly in a hut on the cliff tops watching for shipping; and the hardest part of all the trials he endured in the Navy was being marooned on a ship for months on end with no opportunity to be alone.

The Prince is no hermit. He enjoys the company of others, likes nothing better than a good dinner surrounded by friends, and large noisy get-togethers with his family. His interest in people in the street is very genuine too. He wants to know how they live, how they think. Many are the times he has held up busy working schedules because he has become fascinated by someone he has encountered in a crowd. Polo is a team game, hunting is a gregarious activity, and he uses it as such. He chats to people in the field, remembers faces, and will pick up on topics discussed in a previous

'If I have a game of polo I feel five hundred times better in my mental outlook.' Diana with Charles at a polo match in Melbourne in 1985

conversation. He actively seeks out company at times, but on other occasions he needs to be completely alone. To take stock, to recharge his batteries, and there is no place on earth he would rather do it than in the Highlands of Scotland. He is surrounded there by everything he loves; he can walk for mile upon mile and meet nothing more taxing than the occasional sheep; he can fish one of the best salmon rivers in Britain; he can stalk deer, a sport he finds fascinating as well as challenging; and he can paint. Charles took up watercolour painting nearly twenty years ago, and it has become one of his greatest pleasures.

'The great thing about painting', he says, 'is that it is your *own* individual interpretation of whatever view you have chosen. Because it obliges you to sit down and make a careful observation of the chosen subject, you discover so much more than by just pointing a camera. As a result, you become increasingly more aware of the quality of light and shade, of tone and texture and of the shape of buildings. In short, it has revolutionized my life and, through the requirement of intense concentration, it is one of the most relaxing and therapeutic exercises I know.'

The Prince is genuinely modest about his artistic talent, perpetually apologizes for his amateurishness and longs to be more skilled; and, as with most things, he finds he

Charles and Diana had a very relaxed audience with the Pope on their Italian visit

becomes much better with daily practice. Balmoral is one place where he can do that.

The Prince's other favourite place to paint, and indeed to be, is Italy, which, for all his travels, he had never visited until the spring of 1985. It was a visit filled with promise and excitement, and one that he and the Princess obviously enjoyed. They were going to the home of opera, to listen to some Verdi, Puccini and Donizetti; and to see at first hand the fine art and architecture that he had studied and only previously heard about or seen in books. They were to look at the sculpture of Michelangelo, and the frescoes on the ceiling of the Sistine Chapel. Charles had longed to visit the Basilica in Rome, to see Venice in all its glory; to walk across the Ponte Vecchio in Florence, virtually unchanged since the sixteenth century, and to visit the villages in the Tuscan hills, intact after hundreds of years. He had heard so much about it from the Queen Mother – who as a child had been there every year – and from so many other people that he had felt it was a part of his education that was sorely lacking. The high spot of the tour, however, was to be an audience with the Pope.

Charles had planned to take part in a private Mass with the Pope, but was forbidden at the last moment after strong protest to the government from the Church of England hierarchy. It was an official state visit, so he and the Princess were ruled by the Foreign Office and, in this case, overruled. Charles was intensely angry and upset. He has a deep religious conviction, which tends towards the ecumenical, and this would have been a perfect expression of his beliefs and also a personal and rewarding spiritual experience. It was not to be. Instead, they had a forty-five-minute audience, which Diana was extremely nervous about – more so than at any meeting with any leader before or since. However, it turned out to be a very relaxed meeting, so much so that when the private session was over and the press were invited in to take photographs, the Prince said to the Pope, 'Let me introduce you to my press corps.'

From Rome they flew down to join *Britannia* in Sicily for the remainder of the tour, where the Prince's artist friend John Ward was waiting. 'If my grandmother can take Sir Hugh Casson to Venice,' he had said some months before, 'can I take you?'

Charles had met Ward several years before, and, as well as seeking his advice as a teacher, had commissioned several paintings from him. Shortly before the wedding Edward Adcane, Charles's private secretary, had been in a dining club with the artist; he pushed a packet of cigarettes across the table towards him. Written on the back were the words, 'My boss wants you to draw his wedding'. Not long afterwards came another request, this time in a slightly more orthodox fashion, for John Ward to paint the Princess. He has since painted Prince William's christening and Prince Charles himself, and the portraits all hang in pride of place in the privacy of Kensington Palace and Highgrove.

From Sicily they sailed up the coastline to Venice together. Every day the Prince and Princess went off on official business, to look at churches, visit hospitals and meet people, and the minute they were back on board the royal yacht, Charles would

The deaf children of the Molfetta Deaf School in Trani were proud to have been singled out for a visit by the Princess

quickly change into some comfortable clothes and sit on deck with his sketchbook and teacher, until the very last minute before the bell for dinner.

The trip was a revelation. Diana was not so enthused by the architecture, which Charles delighted in, but there was no doubting the warmth of the welcome – they were greeted everywhere as '*Carlo e De*' – and the sheer beauty of the place and the warm weather lifted everyone's spirits after an English winter. Diana also enjoyed the attentiveness of Italian men, whose appreciation of good-looking women and elegant dressing is second to none. She visited hospitals and schools, even a school for the deaf, where she boasted that she was president of the British Deaf Association. The children didn't understand at first, but when it was later explained to them, they were enormously proud that she should have singled them out for a visit. It was one of the most enjoyable tours they had had. With the prospect of William and Harry joining them for a holiday afterwards, Diana was in good heart.

For the Prince, it was the beginning of a love affair, one that has taken him back to Italy on many occasions. He has found friends there. He stays with the historian Sir Harold Acton, in Florence, and the fabulously rich Frescobaldi family; and spends his time painting and soaking up the culture of the land that bred so many great artists. Last year he was invited to hold an exhibition of his work at Urbino, in central Italy, at the house once owned by the Renaissance painter Raphael, which he had visited a few years before. It was the first time that such an offer had ever been made; initially, he was loath to put his sketches on public display – but he was also flattered. Finally, after some 'agonizing', he agreed 'on the grounds', as he wrote in the introduction to the catalogue, 'that I have a passion for Italy, her people, her countryside and the way in which art quite naturally seems to invade every aspect of life, thereby producing an atmosphere that is totally irresistible'.

He sent the paintings but none were for sale. As he explained in Urbino, 'These sketches are very much a part of myself and I am sure those who paint themselves will understand how hard it is to part with something into which, when inspired, you have poured your heart and soul.' He is also concerned about being unable to control their value on the open market, with individuals making money out of what had originally been a means of raising money for charity.

Sir Hugh Casson had helped Charles and encouraged him with his painting for many years, and is impressed by his skill. He said of the Urbino exhibition:

The works on show are as relaxed as the setting – they speak quietly – no drama, no rhetoric – and their message is clear that The Prince of Wales, like every serious artist, paints not just what he sees but what he *is* . . . a man obviously happiest in the open air, preoccupied (like all Englishmen) with our landscape and our weather (itself as misty, mid-toned and lacking in extremes as the English themselves). He draws inspiration from ordinary scenes and simple places that he knows and loves. He obviously has heeded Ruskin's advice not just to look at things but to 'watch' them.

Diana does not paint, and could not have shared her husband's absorption. Her interests are almost all active ones; and to be with someone whose idea of a holiday is to sit stock still for three hours at a time, with a small box of watercolours and a sketch pad and 'watch' things, was beyond her. Fishing held no appeal for her either. Nothing could be more boring, to her mind, than standing on the banks of a river for hour after hour, sometimes the entire day, hoping for a fish to take. She had neither the patience nor the inclination. Diana needs people; unlike the Prince, she is not much good at being on her own. As a child at Althorp, a big and lonely place where she often had no other children for company, she would go into the kitchen to chatter to the cook and the cleaners, and even the delivery men who dropped in. She loves talking to people, and keeping in touch with what is going on in their lives. As such, she is a compulsive user of the telephone, and rings everyone, especially friends and family. She is also a great letter-writer, a hangover no doubt from years at boarding school, where she had to write to both parents every week. She writes as she speaks, a flow of news and thoughts in large, generous handwriting, with affectionate endings, such as 'Lots of Love' or 'All my love' – even to members of her staff. People are her lifeline; they would have been whoever she had married. She loves the country and Highgrove is home, especially with the children, but she needs to know the city is not too far away, with shops and cinemas and friends to meet up with. The idea of being marooned at Balmoral for months on end is her vision of purgatory.

So after a brief visit to Balmoral in the summer, Diana soon established a pattern of leaving Charles to it and returning to London and her friends. This was quite the most sensible arrangement; it was more fun for the children too. Their friends were either in London or around Gloucestershire, and they had very active social lives, particularly after William started kindergarten in September 1985.

Charles, in the meantime, would invite people who he knew shared his enthusiasms to keep him company. He went off to Italy one year with his cousin and fellow-artist, Lady Sarah Armstrong-Jones. He went fishing with his friends of old, Lord and Lady Tryon. Kanga, as she is better known, was an ex-girlfriend and has remained a trusted friend. Lord and Lady Tryon had a house in Iceland where Charles had frequently been a guest before he was married. In fact, he was fishing on a fiord nearby at the precise moment when his detective brought him the news that Lord Mountbatten had been killed. The Tryons, in return, have frequently joined him for some fishing at Balmoral.

The Prince is also very keen on deer stalking, another pull to keep him in the Highlands for as long as he can manage. He is not especially fond of killing animals but, as a countryman, he sees culling deer as a necessity. If they were allowed to breed at random and each live life to its natural end, in the absence of any real predators, they would overrun the land, destroy the habitat in an ever-desperate search for food, and upset the eco-system. A good stalker only singles out weak animals from a herd, or those that are past their best. Finding the right animal may involve tracking the herd for miles across steep and inhospitable terrain, and waiting

Charles feels the strong pull of the Highlands, but Diana seldom stays for long

patiently for the right opportunity. It is a skilled sport, best done by people who understand and admire their quarry and are fit enough to pursue and outwit it.

This is not one of his solitary pursuits, however. He is usually accompanied by a stalker and gillie, local men who are familiar with the herds and their habits, and who know the country like the back of their hands and can help lead those doing the shooting to the right place. They take ponies to carry the stags down the hill – nevertheless, it can be a long and exhausting day out.

Prince Charles has been deer stalking since he was a child and takes great pride in a clean kill. He finds it far more challenging than shooting either grouse or pheasant, which he has also done plenty of. There have repeatedly been stories that Diana's disapproval had stopped Charles shooting, but these rumours are quite untrue. Diana was brought up with it, just as Charles was, and is a fair shot herself, although she does not shoot any more. She is nevertheless perfectly happy to go out with the guns and take the boys.

The fact was that Charles gave up shooting for a few years because he had simply grown bored with it: it was too easy to blast away overfed birds frightened into the air by a band of beaters. He still joins in the traditional New Year shooting at Sandringham, but, apart from that family outing, he seldom bothers with shooting birds nowadays. If given an invitation to stalk, however, he jumps at it. He is frequently a guest of Colonel Sir Donald Cameron of Lochiel at Achnacarry, his 80,000-acre deer forest near Fort William.

Trudging back one evening, having been out all day and having had no luck, Charles spotted a large heap of rocks on the hillside above them, and asked what it was. Told that it was a fox's cairn, he insisted on climbing up by himself to have a look at it, and was gone for about twenty minutes. Meanwhile, darkness began to fall. When he finally rejoined the others he was carrying several samples of rock, and there was very little light left.

The party still had to cross Loch Arkaig by boat to meet up with his security men who were waiting with a Range Rover, and were clearly becoming worried. They switched on the car's headlights as a beacon; but, all of a sudden, as the Prince and his companions were half-way across the water, the lights swung round and moved away as the vehicle set off down the glen.

When they landed there was no choice but to start the ten-mile journey to Achnacarry Castle on foot, so they set off, even though they had been walking all day. Just then they saw the lights come hurtling back up the rough track towards them. In the confusion of explanations and apologies that followed, one of the security men rounded on the stalker for keeping the Prince out so late. Charles defended the man stoutly, and asked instead, what the hell the driver thought he had been doing careering up and down the lochside like that. 'All you're doing is wasting petrol,' he said.

Another stalking host is Lord King, British Airways supremo, who has a hunting lodge in the Borders. Lord King is a friend from the fox-hunting field, another sport that Charles would defend on the grounds of control and conservation. Farmers encouraging foxes to live on their land encourage a whole range of other wildlife that enjoys the same habitat, as has been done at Highgrove. If the farmers did not want the foxes, they would plough up those areas, and some of those other species might entirely disappear. To which the Prince would add that it is a traditional and historical part of the English way of life, and one that is not, contrary to public opinion, exclusively for the rich. Most hunts are made up of a complete cross-section of society, the only qualification being an ability to ride. Once again, Charles does not hunt because he enjoys killing foxes. He hunts because he finds it exciting to ride a horse at speed and over such unpredictable obstacles. He seldom hunts in Gloucestershire because he finds the large expanses of flat and open farmland boring. So although he has gone to some trouble to leave tracks across his own land at Highgrove specially for the local hunt, the Beaufort, he hardly ever joins them. He much prefers riding with the Quorn in Leicestershire, where there are more hedges and gates to jump. He particularly delights in riding near the front of the field so that he can watch the hounds at work – something that fascinates him.

The Prince's defence of blood sports, which so many of his friends find indefensible, is a curious inconsistency, and one on which he is not keen to be challenged or criticized. Spike Milligan, the ex-Goon, who has been a friend for years, is a veteran anti-blood sports campaigner. He once said that the Royal Family had inherited the problem of hunting and shooting; it was in the blood. The label 'Hunting Junkies' was not well received by his friend, the 'Trainee King'.

10

Searching for a Role

The greatest cause of the Prince's despondency had been the feeling that he served no useful purpose. Friends considered him so depressed during this period that they were even beginning to think the unthinkable – that he might give up and turn his back on society and all its ills, and do what he would have really chosen to do with his life: be a country squire. But in September 1985 he joined forces with a man who was to play a large part in changing all that.

Stephen O'Brien is a remarkable man, liked and respected by everyone he comes into contact with. His main mission in life for the last ten years, as chief executive of an organization called Business in the Community (BitC), has been to cut unemployment and regenerate the inner cities. BitC is a charity, set up in 1981, to breathe life back into Britain's dying towns and cities. It is a partnership between business, central and local government and trade unions, based on the American experience. The idea is simple: communities with high unemployment and economic depression can be turned around if the companies that operate in those communities can be persuaded to become involved in them, invest in them, and train and recruit people from within them. The motivation is self-interest. If the community itself becomes prosperous, the people living in it will have more money to spend on the goods and services being provided by the companies. Everyone benefits.

O'Brien had approached the Prince at the end of 1984 because he wanted support for a particular project, called Fullemploy. It was a training programme for young unemployed blacks in the inner cities, and O'Brien, knowing that Charles already had an interest in this area through the Prince's Trust, thought it was worth seeing if Charles would help.

The Prince was more than keen to help; as a result of that approach he convened a meeting, known as the Windsor Conference, which is still widely regarded as one of the most significant advances ever made in race relations. Between them they brought together in a hotel in Windsor the chairmen of sixty major companies in Britain and a crowd of bright, articulate members of the black community. The black community did the rest. They designed the agenda, ran the conference, and for twenty-four hours the white chairmen were their guests. They mixed, talked and ate together and discussed the problems of unemployment among black youths.

Many people still felt that Diana spent an inordinate amount on clothes

Prince Charles addressed the conference, saying that racism was a problem of the white society and not the black. It was a failure to recognize the potential of the black community and a failure to use it.

The Prince and Stephen O'Brien hit it off well from their first meeting. They shared a common vision, and a very genuine concern for people, their needs, and the quality of their life. O'Brien is much the same age as Charles, and a man of huge industry and enthusiasm whom Charles is able to spark ideas off. He is not impressed by the Prince because of who he is, but because of the man he is: because of his gift for talking to people, his tenacity and his courage in confronting problems that other men would shy away from. The risk that he took in bringing the whole Windsor Conference together was enormous. Nothing of its kind had ever been done before, and it could have blown up in his face.

So when the invitation to become president of BitC arrived shortly afterwards, Charles accepted with alacrity. The invitation could not have come at a better time. He had been hit by a new wave of depression. He and Diana had just returned from an exhausting tour of America, plugging Britain and British industry at every turn. They had endured an embarrassing fund-raising dinner, for which rich Americans had paid 5,000 dollars a ticket, only to discover on their return that the Confederation of British Industry had done nothing to follow it up with any kind of sales drive. 'What's the point?' said Charles. 'I'm no good at anything. It's all a waste of time.'

But BitC was an outfit with drive, enthusiasm, and a determination to make the sort of changes in society that Charles had been trying to make for years. Here were people who shared his ideals and had the financial support of government and industry, while his endeavours had to rely on the begging bowl. And here were people who wanted him not just for the name on the letter-head, but because they thought he could make a positive contribution. Here, as it has turned out, was an organization where he has found he is seriously good at something, and where all the disparate strands of his life have come together with extraordinary clarity.

'The day you think I am not useful,' he said to one of BitC's directors, 'tell me. I want to be involved in the growth of something. I don't just want to open things and be seen trundling around. I can go to all the dinners and banquets on earth, but it's not going to make any difference to the world. What I want to do is be part of something that does.'

Despite his pessimism, the Prince has, of course, made a considerable difference, if not to the world, then certainly to a number of individuals living in it. One such group was the disabled community for whom he had set up the Prince of Wales Advisory Group on Disability. Under the chairmanship of Bill Buchanan – who, like the group's then director, Nancy Robertson, is wheelchair-bound – the committee highlighted five major areas of neglect for disabled people: access, housing, employment, independent living and prevention. They are steadily working through them.

The first was tackled in a way that was to set the pattern – a devastating technique that the Prince has used time and again: bringing people together who would not normally meet. In some cases they may be diametrically opposed. In this instance he invited the top private housebuilders, designers and architects in Britain to a lunch at Kensington Palace, and put them together with members of his advisory group, two of whom were in wheelchairs. They called for four changes in modern house design: sloping paths in the landscaping rather than steps, lower concrete thresholds, wider doors to let wheelchairs through, and a downstairs lavatory.

The result was certainly an improvement. Sir Laurie Barratt of Barratt's Homes set his architects to work at once and, after a few initial hiccups, the message has filtered through.

The Prince of Wales is an irrepressible font of ideas, a classic entrepreneur. In another area, he had long cherished a dream to provide some sort of community service for young people in this country. Most people, he felt, have an altruistic streak in them – irrespective of social background, culture or experience – and they should have the opportunity, at least once in their lives, to work together with others for the benefit of the community. He had watched the effect that team spirit had had on the young people who had been on Operation Drake. Many more youngsters had been dispatched around the world in Operation Raleigh, and he felt there must be a way for every young person to experience these kind of benefits. This was the way. So he wrote to George Thurstan, an ex-marine who was running the Drake Fellowship; this was a scheme set up by the Prince in the wake of the inner-city riots, to give young people from those areas adventure training. Why, asked the Prince, was Britain the only country in Europe that did not have some kind of community service?

The answer was that community service was a political minefield, and had been rejected as unworkable every time it had reared its head. If you put young people to work digging ditches, the argument ran, you were keeping other people out of employment; and what young people needed was not bogus work but real jobs.

It was a red rag to a bull. 'Stop telling me reasons why it can't be done,' the Prince thundered, 'and get on and find a way.' Bureaucracy and red tape make him angrier than almost anything else. 'Set up a pilot scheme,' he demanded. So, doing as they were bid, discussions were duly held with everyone concerned; just six months after the Prince's letter landed on George Thurstan's desk, a pilot scheme opened for business in Sunderland. Twenty-one days later the Prince arrived to see what was going on.

What was going on was such a success that the idea was launched nationwide five years later, in April 1990, as Volunteers.

'It's an opportunity,' says the brochure, 'to spend some time doing voluntary work. It's not for no-hopers. It's not another source of free or cheap labour. It's not for do-gooders. It's not for ethnic minorities, or ethnic majorities. It's not for the unemployed. The handicapped. Or Young Offenders. It's not for anyone in particular. It's for everyone. In general. And that includes you.'

The schemes are locally run on a franchise basis, by voluntary organizations, schools or employers, and the hope is that in the first phase, up to 1993, 10,000 people aged between sixteen and twenty-four – immediately dubbed 'Charlie's Army' by the press – will join full- or part-time programmes of about twelve weeks.

The brochure continues: 'A lot of things will happen to you during your time with the Volunteers. You'll become part of a team. You'll learn new skills. You will probably do things that you have never done before in your life. And may never get the opportunity to do again.'

The activities include befriending the elderly or taking them on day trips, re-creating trails and footpaths in National Parks, organizing and running barge

The greatest cause of Charles's despondency was the feeling that he served no useful purpose

holidays for mentally handicapped children, and 'greening' inner cities by developing disused allotments.

Seeing his ideas – which were greeted with such a chill at first – take off, was a tremendous boost to the Prince of Wales. But that was not until 1990. The gloom and despondency of the 1980s was destined to last a little longer yet.

More trouble appeared in the shape of an ill-judged television film, which Charles and Diana agreed to make for Independent Television News in 1985: seemingly innocuous, with a bland, not to say sycophantic, interviewer in the shape of Sir Alastair Burnet. They allowed the cameras into Kensington Palace and Highgrove but in the space of two evenings' viewing they came perilously close to destroying that magic ingredient that is so essential to the monarchy: its mystique. In times when there are ever-louder grumblings about the money that is spent maintaining the Royal Family, it is imperative that the public has its belief confirmed that they are special, and in some way different from the rest of us. Allowing the public into their homes for a peep at family life, which left us feeling they were not particularly special, was a dangerous gamble that backfired. Showing the Princess in conference with one of her dress designers did nothing to allay the view that she spent an inordinate amount of money on clothes; and broadcasting the Prince's remark that he talked to the flowers in his garden was a bad mistake. What was said tongue-in-cheek was received as confirmation of everything that had gone before: the Prince of Wales was seriously out of his tree.

He can laugh about it now, and has referred to it in many speeches since to very good effect; but at the time it hurt. Not only that, it was brought up time and again by the media and used to undermine the serious work that he was trying so hard to do. Charles bitterly regretted having allowed the cameras in.

But at the time he had no one with the expertise to guide him, and was very easily influenced by the persuasive arguments of the last person he spoke to on any given subject. He lacked the confidence that has come in the last three or four years to make decisions and stick to them. He was also crying out for an efficient office. After Edward Adeane's departure, David Roycroft, who was a career diplomat from the Foreign Office, had held the fort until a successor could be found, but the whole set-up had always been curiously amateurish. The right hand never knew what the left was doing. People got through to the Prince who should not have, and those who should have didn't. Letters were lost, and time and again Charles would discover that his staff had failed to show him a document or letter, or turned down an invitation on his behalf without ever showing it to him.

When Adeane left, Charles had definite ideas about the sort of man he wanted to replace him, but it was six months before the right man could be found. He wanted someone of high calibre, with business and administrative skills, who was outside the traditional courtier mould yet compatible with the Old Guard already *in situ*. Most important of all, he wanted someone who was sympathetic to his views and who would not be over-protective. The difficulty was that a man of this calibre would almost certainly have to be prepared to take a substantial drop in salary. No one gets rich working for the Royal Family. It was a headhunter who found Sir John Riddell, a successful investment banker in his early fifties.

The Prince needed sound advice, particularly as he moved into more and more controversial areas. He could not afford to make mistakes; all his life he had been at pains to learn and understand how ordinary people live and had delved into the seamier side of human nature, but he was still very unworldly. He was surprised to find, for example, that men who make their living out of reporting news and gossip should go away from a private lunch with him and the Princess and talk about it. He was even more baffled when he tried to convert some of his Duchy property in Kennington into small units for single teenagers – a group that finds it notoriously difficult to find accommodation – and met with vociferous local anger. It took the left-wing blunt Liverpudlian Cathy Ashton, at BitC, to explain it to him.

'The trouble is,' she said, 'that you are inevitably in the position of people being able to say, "It's all right for you, you don't have to live next door to those punks and weirdos." ' Charles had simply thought he was being philanthropic.

Again, on the flight home from Melbourne at the end of their Australian tour in 1985, Charles hand-wrote a long and frank letter about his thoughts on a wide range of issues, including the Greater London Council – a politically explosive subject – and had entrusted it to the common mail, without apparently thinking it unwise. And he once passed on to BitC an invitation he had received requesting him and the Princess to open the conference of a Brent Women's Association, with a note saying, 'Do you think I should do it? C.' The answer was a categorical no: one of the items on the agenda was 'Police Brutality in Brent'.

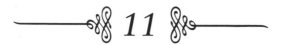

A Rocky Patch

Charles and Diana may not have had many interests in common when they first met, but one that they did have, and have enjoyed together throughout their marriage, is skiing. But yet again, this was another area of their lives that was mismanaged. Given the media's obsession with Diana, it was hardly likely that they would allow the couple the luxury of a week alone in the snow. Somebody should have seen the inevitable scramble coming, but no one did.

The result was chaos: their first skiing holiday ruined by the press, who turned the icy mountain roads of Liechtenstein, where they were staying, into a re-run of the Monte Carlo rally. To escape the posse of photographers and television crews that were always lying in wait, they would set off at high speed along treacherous tracks, with Europe's press in hot pursuit.

The lesson was learned, and in subsequent years a photocall has been organized for the first day, when the Prince and Princess pose sweetly for the cameras on the understanding that thereafter the media will go home so the two can holiday in peace.

They were posing for just such a photocall at Klosters in February 1986, when the photographers suddenly noticed another figure standing in the background, dressed in a Davy Crockett-style fur headband. 'It's Fergie,' someone said, and within seconds Charles and Diana were left staring at an empty patch of snow where a moment before dozens of photographers had been elbowing one another for the best position. They had lit upon Sarah Ferguson instead, who was hotly tipped to be announcing her engagement to Prince Andrew any day, and her appearance in Klosters was their dream come true.

So was it Diana's. If her own marriage had been the result of some matchmaking, so too was Andrew's marriage to Sarah later that year. She herself was principal matchmaker.

Diana had met Fergie through polo. Sarah's father, Major Ronald Ferguson, is Charles's polo manager, so she was frequently at Smith's Lawn, the Guards' Club in Windsor Great Park, where Charles was based, and inevitably she and Diana often sat chatting while the Prince played polo. Fergie was not, strictly speaking, Diana's type; she was certainly not like her old friends, nor indeed many of the friends she has

made in the last few years. She was larger than life, she had seen the world, she was game for anything, she was jolly and vibrant, spoke her mind; all in all, she was fun to be with. Having known the Royal Family all her life, she was easy to talk to, and was one of the few people who knew what Diana was talking about when she spoke about her day-to-day life. In short, they became friends, and as time passed Diana thought her a good match for her errant brother-in-law.

It worked, and at first it seemed a perfect arrangement. Everyone seemed to like Fergie; she was so natural, so unspoilt, and she brought a breath of fresh air wafting through the corridors of Court. For Diana, it was like having an ally in the camp, and Balmoral was much more enjoyable that year with Fergie about. She was not alone any more in feeling oppressed by the strict formality, the strict time-keeping; after-dinner games were more lively – and she was no longer the only one who wanted to giggle at the sound of the bagpipes that played them out of the dining-room after dinner every night.

To begin with, Sarah Ferguson deflected the attentions of the media too. But as time passed, she became a dangerous influence. Emboldened by what she saw her friend get away with, Diana felt able to loosen the shackles a little. She had been in the royal straitjacket for five years and, like most women who marry and have children when they are very young, she began to realize what she had been missing out on. Without Fergie's influence, for example, she would never have gone along to the Berkeley Square night club, Annabel's, as she did on the night of Prince Andrew's stag party, with Fergie and comedienne Pamela Stephenson, both of them dressed up as policewomen. It was unusual company for her to keep in any event: delightful though Pamela Stephenson may be, her public image is not altogether regal, and Charles has always recognized the need to choose his friends, particularly those in showbusiness, with care. Before Fergie appeared, Diana would never have poked an umbrella into the rump of a gentleman friend at Ascot. She might have done it in private – she is fun and playful and, without question, a little flirtatious – but Diana had understood from the start that her public image had to be beyond reproach, and it always had been. Now she appeared to be unconcerned what

Diana met Sarah Ferguson through polo, and they became firm friends

One thing they have enjoyed together throughout their marriage is skiing. In Liechtenstein in 1985

people thought. She was spotted driving about London late at night on her own, having apparently slipped out without her detective. It was the paparazzi who trailed her, but it could so easily have been terrorists.

The tide of affection in which the public had held Diana since she first came to their notice had begun to turn. They began to criticize and mutter doubts about the stability of the fairy-tale marriage. By 1987 she and Charles seemed to have reached an all-time low, if not in their marriage, then certainly in the public's perception of it. It began in Klosters again, with the famous photocall, this time a foursome of the Waleses and the Yorks, ending with Diana and Fergie wrestling to push the other off balance. With Diana in the snow, Charles looked distinctly unamused and drew the session to a close. There were reports of Diana playing tricks on Charles too – changing jackets with a friend, so he would attempt to take home the wrong woman; and there were reports that he spent his evenings at home in the chalet while Diana danced the night away with friends in a disco.

The Princess left Klosters on her own. Back in London, her name began appearing in the gossip columns. She had been, it seemed, to endless dinners, parties and weddings on her own, she had been spotted at local cinemas with friends, sitting in the stalls alongside ordinary members of the public, and she had been seen on the town, at pop concerts, and in restaurants, with handsome young men. Two names in particular appeared with enough regularity for people to talk. That of Philip Dunn, a City banker; and cavalry officer David Waterhouse, a major in the Lifeguards.

The fact that in every instance she was chaperoned, at least by a detective and usually by a group of other friends too, never seemed relevant. The tabloids seemed hell-bent on knocking Diana off the pedestal they had put her on, determined to prove, or invent if necessary, that she had a roving eye.

In April the Prince went off to the Kalahari Desert for a few days with Sir Laurens van der Post, to see for himself the society that his friend had written and talked about so much. No sooner had he come back than he left Diana and the children at home yet again, and went to Italy on a week's painting holiday. Rumours that the marriage was in trouble were gaining substance, particularly when by the end of the summer the press had calculated that Charles and Diana had spent only one day in six weeks together. He had been in Scotland with Kanga, so they said. Diana had been in London with the children, leading a hectic social life. On the one occasion when they had met in those six weeks, it had been to visit flood victims in Wales, in the town of Carmarthen, which had been hit by the freak October hurricane. Charles flew down from Aberdeen, Diana arrived from Highgrove; but instead of going home together, at least for the night, they went their separate ways. By the end of the year even the serious newspapers were discussing the constitutional implications of divorce.

Once again there seemed to be no one around the Prince and Princess with the foresight to see that the situation was becoming seriously out of control. A simple statement to explain why Charles was staying away so long would have been better than nothing. Left with nothing, the press could only draw the conclusion that the marriage was indeed close to disintegration. All they needed was the proof, and when a photographer hired by a down-market Sunday newspaper caught the Princess of Wales emerging from her friend Kate Menzies's mews house during the early hours of the morning with David Waterhouse, and fooling around in the quiet road, they thought they had it. Diana was distraught. She and her detective rushed over to the photographer and she pleaded with him to hand over his film, and tell nothing of what he had seen. He surrendered the film, but, not surprisingly, he went straight back to the newspaper and the story was headline news.

That was the turning point. The Princess was given a serious fright. She had been having a little innocent fun. It was a way of releasing some of the strain and tension of her life. She enjoyed being with her friends; their conversation was lively and interesting, they belonged to the real world – the world she had left behind. She could relax with them and pretend for a while that she was still one of them. She was flattered by their attention and affection, but it was wholly innocuous. She knew that, and Charles knew that, but the public were evidently beginning to think otherwise.

The public, of course, had only the word of the press to guide them, and although there was more than a germ of truth in what the tabloids reported, this was by no means the first autumn in which the Prince had spent weeks without his wife and children. Ever since William had started school, Diana had had to be based in the south. Charles had chosen to stay in Scotland because it was the perfect time of year for all the activities he enjoyed there. It was not pure holiday. Paperwork and a fleet of secretaries and staff go with him wherever he goes, and Balmoral is no exception. So his remaining north of the border for the autumn of 1987 was no indication, in itself, of the state of their marriage.

The Prince was infuriated by the reports. He had long since given up reading the tabloids. As he explained when I met him, he became so angry when he read what they had to say about the Princess that he wanted to ring the editors and complain, but realized that, rather than spending every day on the telephone, a simpler solution was to stop reading them. For some years, therefore, he has only read *The Times*. But even *The Times* was giving space to the possible consequences of a royal divorce.

It made him even more depressed. What right did anybody have to hold forth about his marriage? What business was it of theirs anyway? This was the final straw. He felt that he had given enough. For thirty-nine years he had devoted himself to the British public. He had been through hell in the course of duty; he had made sacrifices that would be asked of no other human being. He had been made an object of fun and a target for abuse. He was wrong whatever he did. If he spoke out, he was accused of poking his nose into matters he knew nothing about; if he stayed out of it, he was accused of slacking and taking too many holidays. He was ridiculed for his speeches, and mocked for his concern about the inner cities. Most hurtful and unfair of all, though, he had been the butt of jokes about his appearance for as long as he could remember – everything from his ears to his hairline.

For Diana, coping with the life she had taken on, and with motherhood, was simply too much

He had had to fight for everything he had done, fight the people who wanted to wrap him up safely and wheel him out for a bit of ribbon-cutting and ceremonial. It would have been a lot easier to have done nothing. His job as Prince of Wales, after all, was simply a job of waiting and preparing to become sovereign. He could have followed in the footsteps of some of his more notorious predecessors, by gambling, drinking and scandalizing society. Or he could have opted out altogether. What he had done, he had done because he wanted to make some contribution, pay back to society the great debt he felt by being born to such privilege.

He had given everything he had. Was it too much to ask that he be allowed some privacy in his life? If his marriage was in trouble it was because he and Diana had not been given a chance. His wife had been plagued by the press from the beginning, and coping with the stress of it all was simply too much.

Nevertheless, the fact that the matter had come to such a head did have a sobering effect on them both. The press had no right to pry and push and sneak about in their private lives, but it was undeniable that if their marriage were to fail, it would open up an entire can of constitutional worms that the monarchy could well do without. Their marriage was not like anyone else's. They could not afford to let it fall apart.

Braving the cameras and the columnists, and the experts who'd been brought in to analyse every glance and nuance of their body language, they faced the world, and slowly worked at healing the rift between them.

12

Saving the Environment

When an organization invites the Prince or Princess of Wales to make a speech on their behalf, it is customary for them to write a draft, incorporating any appropriate facts and figures or particular message that they want conveyed in the speech.

The Department of the Environment provided just such a draft when they invited the Prince, as the United Kingdom's patron of the European Year of the Environment, to open the Second International Conference on the Protection of the North Sea in November 1987. It was a prestigious event, attended by ministers and top delegates from all over Europe, and the speech delivered to the Prince's office was straightforward and bland, essentially a pat on the back for Britain in all she was doing to keep the North Sea clean.

The Department had underestimated their speaker, and in so doing had made an embarrassing mistake. Charles took one look at the proffered platitudes, which he knew to be absurd, and set about writing an alternative. As with his architectural assaults, he trawled for information from a wide range of experts in the environmental field, including the pressure group Friends of the Earth, whose director at that time was Jonathon Porritt. Armed with some facts and figures, he confidentially approached a number of very senior civil servants within the Department of the Environment. All the advice he had been getting, he told them, was that Britain was in fact very culpable in North Sea pollution issues. The speech he had been given was way off the mark, and he would like the truth.

The truth he got, but, when he rose to his feet at the splendid Queen Elizabeth II Conference Centre to declare the summit open, no more than a few people present had any inkling of what he was about to say. The Secretary of State, Nicholas Ridley, was certainly not one of them.

The Prince spoke as follows:

The North Sea was once one of Europe's great highways. This 'silver sea' was also, and still is, one of the world's richest fishing zones – as well as a playground for sailors and a source of inspiration for poets and painters.

But over the past century we have made it into a rubbish dump. The effluents we

pour heedlessly into its waters are a threat to its delicate ecological balance.

Some argue that we do not have enough proof of danger to justify stricter controls on dumping or to warrant the extra expenditure involved. They say we must wait for science to provide that proof. If science has taught us anything, however, it is that the environment is full of uncertainty. It makes no sense to test it to destruction. While we wait for the doctor's diagnosis the patient may easily die.

We do not have a lot of time left in which to act . . . We know enough to know that these things are not good for our life support system or for our quality of life, and that our activities have damaging effects on our wildlife.

Therefore, how we decide to use our oceans and waterways in future is probably one of the most important choices for this particular generation.

The Prince could not have hoped for a better platform. The effect was explosive, and deeply embarrassing to the government's position, which for years had been obstructive – to such an extent that Britain had long been known as 'The Dirty Man of Europe'. Demands for action to clean up sulphur dioxide emissions from power stations, widely believed to be responsible for the 'acid rain' that was killing forests, lakes and rivers – not just in Scotland, but as far afield as Germany and Scandinavia – were brushed aside on the grounds of inconclusive evidence; a similar attitude was taken towards the radioactive discharges from the nuclear reprocessing plant at Sellafield. The government had never been prepared to take any action without incontrovertible proof of a direct relationship between an industrial process and a particular pattern of death, disease or environmental damage. If the Prince of Wales had not stood up and spoken as he did that day, the government might have remained entrenched on the subject for considerably longer than it was.

It was something of a turning point for the Prince too. He had trod a very narrow path, fraught with danger; had he been wrong on any detail, it would have spelt disaster. Speaking his mind about the medical profession, even waging war on the architectural establishment, was a very different matter from denouncing the government's attitude to pollution. He had come close to the mark in his various schemes for the inner cities, but he had always taken great care not to overstep the boundary. It was imperative, as he knew, not to get embroiled in politics, and he had been utterly furious when it appeared that architect Rod Hackney had done it for him. In October 1985 the *Manchester Evening News* ran a story, immediately picked up elsewhere, that Charles had confided in Hackney about his fears for the future, of a country divided into the 'haves' and the 'have-nots', of 'no-go' inner-city areas, and racial minorities alienated from the rest of society. Charles was in Australia when this particular bomb dropped, but he still felt the full effect of the fall-out. There were angry calls from Buckingham Palace and Downing Street and, in the House of Commons, Labour's Shadow Home Secretary was treating it as a gift from heaven.

Charles nearly always re-writes the speeches that are prepared for him

The Queen is a proud mother, but sometimes she feels Charles is too outspoken

The North Sea summit was a first. The Prince had never publicly been so outspoken on such a politically sensitive subject, but it was something he felt he could not ignore. He believed it was his duty to speak out. He has devoted time and energy to people because it is the people who will one day be his subjects, and he feels a sense of responsibility towards them; but he will also be King of the British Isles, and has a responsibility to safeguard those Isles for future generations. Everything he had seen, read and heard told him that Britain was in grave danger from the excesses of industrialization, and nothing very significant was being done to halt the process. The problem had not appeared overnight; he was not leaping feet first into a situation that he had not thought about. Prince Charles had been talking and gently agitating about the subject for many years. It was now seventeen years since the Countryside in 1970 Conference, when he had talked about 'the horrifying effects of pollution in all its cancerous forms'. It was all those problems, and a few more, that were now fouling up the North Sea and other parts of Britain. His North Sea assault gave the environmentalists a powerful and unique spokesman; it made the government sit up and take notice; and it speeded up the long and painful process of making the public aware that there was a very real problem to solve, which was going to involve personal sacrifices.

Another instance of Charles's outspokenness was his attack on the proposed Paternoster Square development. This turned him into a hero of the silent majority. He discovered that night, in what has been called his 'Luftwaffe' speech, that his was not a voice in the wilderness; instead, he was speaking for the man on the Clapham omnibus. The occasion was the annual dinner of the Corporation of London's Planning and Communication Committee at the Mansion House, when Charles seized the opportunity to say a few words about the plans for the redevelopment of Paternoster Square. This is the area to the north of St Paul's Cathedral, where there is a 1950s development, which he described as 'the prototype for all the windswept urban squares dreamt up in the fifties and sixties' that amounted to 'the rape of

THIS FOUNDATION STONE
FOR THE SAINSBURY WING
OF THE NATIONAL GALLERY
WAS LAID BY
THEIR ROYAL HIGHNESSES
E PRINCE AND PRINCESS OF V
ON 30 MARCH 1988

Charles's attacks on modern architecture made him a hero of the silent majority. After attacking earlier plans, he laid the foundation stone of the National Gallery extension

Britain'. The whole lot was to come down and make way for a million square feet of office space, and the company developing the site had held a competition to find a master-planner. Seven architectural practices were invited to enter, and it was awarded to Arup Associates. Charles had been given a view of the plans some months before and had been appalled. 'I must confess I was deeply depressed,' he said later. 'It didn't seem to rise to the occasion. This site is next to our great national cathedral – the very heart of the capital city. What place in Britain could be more important? This was something that I felt I had to speak up about.'

Speak up he did, to dramatic effect. As he began his speech, his hosts at the Mansion House dinner looked on in disbelief:

It is not just *me* who is complaining. Countless people are appalled by what has happened to their capital city, but feel totally powerless to do anything about it.

What have we done to St Paul's since the bombing? In the space of a mere fifteen years, in the sixties and seventies, and in spite of all sorts of elaborate rules supposedly designed to protect that great view, your predecessors, as the planners, architects and developers of the City, wrecked the London skyline and desecrated the dome of St Paul's. Not only did they wreck the London skyline in general. They also did their best to lose the great dome in a jostling scrum of office buildings, so mediocre that the only way you ever remember them is by the frustration they induce.

Can you imagine the Italians walling in St Mark's in Venice or St Peter's in Rome?

You have, Ladies and Gentlemen, to give this much to the Luftwaffe: when it knocked down our buildings, it didn't replace them with anything more offensive than rubble. We did that. Large numbers of us in this country are getting fed up of being talked down to and dictated to by the existing planning, architectural and development establishment.

And at street level, just look at Paternoster Square. Did modern planners and architects in London ever use their eyes?

Surely here, if anywhere, was the time and place to sacrifice some profit. If need be, for generosity of vision, for elegance, for dignity; for buildings which would raise our spirits and our faith in commercial enterprise, and prove that capitalism can have a human face.

The Prince had become older and wiser since his previous attacks. He had considered what he would say long and hard, he had had discussions with a wide variety of architects, planners and journalists, eighteen of whom had attended a meeting at Highgrove in September. He had trawled for views and ideas, as has become his method. At least twenty-five professionals made an input to the speech.

It caused a furore nevertheless. Most of the architectural establishment were outraged, and lost no time in condemning the Prince. They did not mince their words. One developer said his speech was 'as welcome as a bad smell in a space capsule'. The architect Richard MacCormac said, 'I believe there is a danger that classicism is being used as a cure-all architectural pill, when architecture has got a lot more to it than just putting in columns and capitals. If Prince Charles wants to go on in this exhorting role, he has to understand architecture.' Richard Rogers described the Prince's actions as 'very vicious – and very questionable democratically'. The best way to deal with him was 'to starve him of the oxygen of publicity'.

'As I anticipated,' the Prince said, 'there was rather an interesting row after I said all that. But it instantly became clear that I wasn't speaking just for myself.'

What Charles craved was a return to classical architecture, to buildings that were sympathetic to their surroundings, that were well proportioned and sensitive to human feelings, and not purely functional. Of the Paternoster Square development, what he wanted to see, he said, was 'a roofscape that gives the impression that St Paul's is floating above it like a great ship in the sea'.

Waiting in the wings, as he knew, was just such a scheme, which had been produced by a young architect called John Simpson. A plan of it had appeared in the

Architects' Journal the previous Friday, and it also appeared in *The Times* the morning after the Prince's speech.

At that time classical architecture was largely confined to the world of country-house building, and the majority of architects exhibiting were older men. By 1987, however, the classical style of architecture had started being used on large-scale developments also, and the average age of the architects doing this kind of work had dropped. Over half the exhibitors were in their thirties and forties, an age that was becoming of increasing significance to the Prince. He was greatly cheered to find so many young architects designing the new classical buildings of which he so much approved.

John Simpson had also been appalled by the competition entries for Paternoster Square and, at a very late stage, had managed to get hold of a copy of the brief – to provide office space and car parking – and had sat down with a number of colleagues to draw up a scheme of their own. The Arup scheme had been a modernist design, which essentially built a wall around St Paul's and squeezed in as much office space as possible behind it. John Simpson and his associates wanted to try and reunite the cathedral with the rest of the City. Any new buildings, they felt, must relate to the cathedral and be a part of the City. Initially, they simply put together a series of guidelines, concerned with scale, height and the street network between the buildings, which amounted to two sheets of paper that they sent to the developer. Nothing came of it; the developers were not interested in the Simpson ideas.

Undeterred, Simpson went on to produce an 'alternative' scheme, which, thanks to the Prince's involvement in bringing the whole issue into the open, went on public display alongside models of all the official proposals in the crypt of St Paul's Cathedral. The Arup scheme held centre stage, but the public, whose views were for once solicited, showed a very definite preference for the Simpson plan. It became a matter for public debate, newspaper articles were written, television programmes made, and the London *Evening Standard* sponsored Simpson's planning application to the City. Neither Arup nor the developers stood a chance.

The site has changed hands several times since then. It is now owned by the Paternoster Association, which is made up of British, American and Japanese interests. It now seems certain that St Paul's Cathedral will not be surrounded by a modernist wall, but by a sympathetic series of buildings in the best classical tradition.

13

Relating

It would perhaps be too trite to pretend that the Prince and Princess's marriage was saved by Diana's involvement with Relate (formerly called the Marriage Guidance Council). It certainly might have helped Diana to listen and learn from counselling sessions, where other couples' problems are aired and discussed; but there is no doubt that by taking on the role of patron at a time when the world was prophesying doom for her own marriage was an exceptionally brave thing for her to do.

As 1988 progressed it became obvious that Diana had matured immeasurably. She had relaxed, and found new confidence. She seemed to have come down to earth, leaving behind the soap-opera image that she had once appeared to be caught up in. Any whiff of scandal had evaporated, and she now threw herself into a hectic work schedule. So too did the Prince. The various strands of his life were beginning to come together. He had plunged into the den of architects once more, and been suitably bloodied. He had also set the cat among the pigeons on the environmental issue. The relationship with BitC was working well and, as he began his fortieth year, the future was looking positive.

It was the start of a new improved relationship between the royal couple. Whatever had gone on in those weeks apart, whatever course of action their friends had counselled, a minor transformation had occurred. The warm familiarity was back, and they appeared to find pleasure and amusement in each other's company.

A trip to Australia for the country's bicentennial celebrations was a good start to the year. Diana not only ostentatiously wore outfits that she had been seen in before – to knock a few criticisms on the head about the money she spent on her wardrobe – but she also seized the opportunity to kill off a few more misconceptions. Visiting a music school in Melbourne, the royal couple looked in on a cello class that was in full swing, supervised by a delightful seventy-eight-year-old professor, Henri Touzeau. Knowing the Prince played the cello, the professor asked whether he would like to have a go. Charles had once been able to play quite proficiently, but was very out of practice. He had taken up the cello at Gordonstoun, when his housemaster, Bob Whitby, could stand the noise of the bagpipes – his chosen instrument – no longer.

For Diana to become Patron of Relate was an exceptionally brave thing to do when the world was prophesying doom for her own marriage

Listening to counsellors help others no doubt helped their marriage. Visiting a Relate centre in Worcester

'No, not at all, thank you,' said the Prince, and, even when pressed by the professor, he would not be moved. So the professor turned his attention to Diana, and invited her to play the piano. Scarcely pausing for thought, she sat herself down at the keyboard and, without so much as a sheet of music to look at, launched into Rachmaninov's Second Piano Concerto, blushing deeply to the round of spontaneous applause. The professor was filled with praise. The Princess, he declared, was 'very accomplished, a very sensitive player and shows great musical ability. She played with such warmth.' Her grandmother would have been proud. Before she was married, Ruth, Lady Fermoy, trained as a concert pianist under Albert Cortot at the Paris Conservatoire.

It certainly knocked the 'Disco Di' image firmly on the head. Not only does Diana play the piano at home, she invariably has a background of classical music playing in her sitting-room and in her private study. At a gala concert of the Philharmonia Orchestra to inaugurate an International Conference on Cancer Nursing, she was sitting in the dark of the Royal Festival Hall playing the movements on an imaginary piano on her knees. Her taste has changed as she has grown older. She still likes pop music, especially the singers and groups she grew up with, like Neil Diamond, Dire Straits and Duran Duran, and thoroughly enjoys the rock concerts she attends, but she now finds classical music more soothing to read and work to. Also, she is busy educating herself about opera.

When Diana became patron of the Welsh National Opera, one of the original five patronages she took on when she became Princess of Wales, she confessed that she did not know very much about opera – and that her principal love was ballet. 'But my husband is going to teach me,' she said, 'and I am going to teach him about ballet.'

With this in mind, she had taken Charles with her when she went to see them perform for the first time. It was a production of *Carmen*, at the Dominion Theatre in London in December 1983. Although based in Cardiff, the Welsh National Opera tours extensively, and for the last twelve years has had a regular season in London too. This was an ambitious, complex production, and, thanks to a particularly officious fire officer, it teetered on the brink of disaster. It gave Brian McMaster, the company's managing director, the worst night he has ever had.

The fire officer inspected the set at about 6 o'clock on the evening of the performance, as fire officers normally do, to put a flame to the scenery to ensure it is properly fire-proofed. The same produc-

Diana's principal love has always been ballet. At a Bolshoi ballet performance in London

tion had been playing in six or seven theatres in Britain already, and no fire officer in any of those places had found any problem. This fire officer, however, refused to allow the use of a sizeable proportion of the props, around which the entire show was structured; and, although the Prince and Princess of Wales were arriving in one and a half hours' time along with five Cabinet ministers, and the cast would have no time to rehearse without the props they relied upon, he was not to be budged.

'Everyone's concentration on stage completely went,' recalls Brian McMaster with a nervous chuckle. 'It was the worst performance we have ever given. That night must have set the arts in Britain back years. The Princess was very kind though. She said she enjoyed it.'

She also went up on to the stage afterwards to meet the singers, and endeared herself to them all when one of the chorus asked, 'Why don't you come and audition for the company?'

'Well, my husband says I've got rather a good voice,' she responded.

That has yet to be tested in public, but the evening certainly did not put her off – she has been an ardent fan of the Welsh National Opera ever since. She has also made a concerted effort to improve her knowledge. Her old flatmate Carolyn Pride, who has since married and become Carolyn Bartholomew, has been instrumental in this. She is extremely musical. She was studying at the Royal College of Music when she moved into Coleherne Court with Diana, and then went on to become an opera singer, pausing only recently to have a couple of children. She has taken Diana to Covent Garden on innumerable occasions in the last few years. They go quite privately; they buy tickets for the Grand Tier and, although a detective goes too, no one knows the Princess of Wales is in the house until they find themselves sitting behind her.

Diana much prefers sitting in the body of the auditorium where she can see what is going on on stage. In most theatres, including Covent Garden, the view from the Royal Box is one of the worst in the house. She prefers the auditorium, even when she is there in an official capacity, as John Young, chairman of the National Hospital, discovered to his dismay.

The Princess had become patron of the hospital, where her father made his miraculous recovery after his cerebral haemorrhage in 1978, and in May 1988 she had agreed to attend a gala performance of *The Magic Flute* at the London Coliseum. John Young, a larger-than-life figure, had automatically assumed the Princess would sit in the Royal Box, and had sold tickets in the belief that everyone in the theatre would have a view of the Princess. No, he was firmly told, the Princess would sit in the Dress Circle. He protested. People were coming from all over the country to see her, and anyone sitting at the back of the stalls or the upper circle would not catch a glimpse. 'I got a bloody nose over that,' he says. 'I was told to mind my own business.'

It was a demonstration of Diana's new-found confidence. At one time she might have wanted to sit among the crowd, to escape from the prying eyes, but she would never have had the confidence to say so. Her assurance has obviously come with age and experience, but there is no doubt that her first major public speech marked a turning point.

It was the day she received the Freedom of the City of London, at the Guildhall in July 1987 – a terrifying ordeal by anyone's standards. She had to stand up in the midst of a certain amount of pomp and ceremony and address a large audience, which included her own family, her husband, the Prime Minister, the Lord Mayor and a host of City dignitaries, many of them accomplished public speakers themselves.

In the early days Diana had had some guidance from Sir Richard Attenborough. He had been able to teach her some of the ploys that actors use to control their breathing when they are nervous, and project their voices so they can be heard. For the past six years, however, she had done little more than declare things open, or say a few words of thanks in public. It was clear that she had picked up a lot from the Prince's own style, especially the self-deprecating wit. Diana began her speech:

I am rather unsure of my qualifications for such an honour, but I feel deeply grateful and flattered to be joining the many famous people who have received the Freedom of this great City, including my more illustrious and worthy ancestor, the third Earl Spencer. I know my Spencer ancestors built their wealth in the sixteenth century on the rearing of sheep, and I believe one of the benefits of receiving the Freedom of the City is that Freemen, or Women, are able to drive sheep across London Bridge and through the City of London. I promise I will give you good warning before I avail myself of this privilege.

My connections with the City are, as I have said, rather tenuous, but it is nearly six years ago to the day since our wedding, when yet again the traffic in the City was brought to a standstill. Since that July day I have visited the City on numerous occasions . . . connected directly or indirectly to asking the City for help with fund-raising. Perhaps now is an opportunity of thanking everyone for their generosity and to say how greatly I know it is appreciated by the charities and organizations concerned.

'Be always ready, according to your power to relieve the poor and help the distressed . . .' is a quote from *The Rules for the Conduct of Life*, a copy of which is given to all new Freemen – or perhaps it should now be Freepersons.

Sitting in the audience was Diana's father, Earl Spencer, who had always been very proud of his daughter, and only too happy to tell the world so. 'She's very genuine, she's very beautiful and she's still very much in love with Prince Charles,' he told *Woman's Own*, in a bid to rebut rumours that the marriage was in trouble. 'Charles and Diana have their rows,' he said, 'what couple doesn't? But they are nothing out of the ordinary.' Of the rumours, he said, 'Diana finds them very hurtful because they are not true.' And on the other burning question that was asked time and time again – whether she will have more children – he said, digging an even deeper hole for himself:

'She'd love a large family because she knows the joys of it. She likes the atmosphere of a large family. I'm quite sure she'd like to have several more children yet – five seems a good number.

'There are times when I wish she could have a couple of years off to bring up her children, be at home with them, and not worry about anything else apart from them and her husband. Instead, it's a bit like a non-stop circus.'

'She'd love a large family because she knows the joys of it.'

Royal reporters have been speculating on a new pregnancy for years, and members of the public have been no less nosy. Visiting Aberdeen one day a woman in the crowd said, 'When are you going to have another baby?'

'I'll have to ask my husband about that,' replied the Princess.

There have been several false alarms in the tabloids, but at the end of 1986 reporters thought they had a scoop. It was during Diana's trip to the Gulf with the Prince, when they suddenly spotted her obstetrician, George Pinker, in Bahrain, among the guests at an official dinner. But Diana was equally surprised. 'George, what are you doing here?' she asked. The answer was that he had flown out quite coincidentally to attend a wedding.

The Princess would like more children. She would dearly love some daughters to be able to pass her jewellery on to and, coming from a large family, she enjoys the atmosphere that plenty of children create. The Prince would no doubt also like to have more children, but he is very torn over the question of population control. Having witnessed the horrifying poverty and hunger in countries where there is just not enough food to feed the teeming masses, he feels depressed and worried about the future. In most areas of life, he tries to practise what he preaches.

The Prince and Princess had both been on particularly good form throughout that Gulf tour, and were reduced to giggles on several occasions, none more so than during a desert picnic. Wherever they went a box of Kleenex tissues lay in wait for Diana, and for Charles, a mysterious red briefcase. And there in the middle of the desert, in a tent hung with Persian carpets, were the ubiquitous tissues and the briefcase. Opening it up Charles found a telephone inside, but was still none the wiser.

They were both on particularly good form throughout the Gulf tour of November 1986

Diana has always been in danger of getting the giggles at the least appropriate moment

Diana has always been in danger of getting the giggles at the least appropriate moment, and age has done very little to cure her. The smallest thing can set her off, and the customs in the Middle and Far East did not help. In the Gulf, in addition to the Kleenex, everywhere they went, no matter what time of day, they were given little cups of very strong coffee to drink. In Japan, the custom of taking their shoes off everywhere, sitting on the floor to eat, and having an elaborate tea ceremony at every port of call, finally cracked her up. In Thailand, in 1988, she and Prince Charles once again had to go barefoot.

Charles has had years of practice and had already encountered all the customs and forms of national dress that amuse Diana so much. But his sense of the absurd is no less than hers. For most of his life he has been stuck with a reputation for finding the Goons funny, but nothing since that era. Far from it. He and Diana attended the gala opening of Barry Humphries' show, *Back With A Vengeance*, in aid of the Royal Marsden Hospital, and both were in hysterics. In it, Humphries plays his outrageous Australian creation, Dame Edna Everage, and Prince Charles kept slapping his knees with merriment and rocking with laughter. Also, at the Gala Night of a Hundred Stars evening at the Mayflower Theatre in Southampton, a mime artist came on stage and found himself struggling with a sticky audience. His humour was just not working. Suddenly, great guffaws of laughter that went on and on broke the silence, so much so that people began to stretch forward to see who they were coming from. It was none other than the heir to the throne, blissfully unaware, and convulsed with mirth.

14

The Wishing Well Appeal

The Princess of Wales is never kept waiting. It is simply not etiquette. Elaborate arrangements are made everywhere she goes, with split-second timing, to ensure that there are no embarrassing hold-ups. Father Christmas, however, operates in much the same way, and when both celebrities were planning to meet up, in December 1987, to deliver Christmas presents to sick children at Great Ormond Street Children's Hospital, there was no competition. The Princess stood out in the cold and waited.

The year before, she and the Prince of Wales had been sent an unusual gift. It was a book, specially written, printed and bound, the only one of its kind, about the historical links between Great Ormond Street Children's Hospital and the Royal Family. The old Victorian hospital, which has performed miracles on thousands of sick children from all over the world in the intervening years, had reached the end of its life. Some £30 million was needed to rebuild it, and the hospital was planning a massive appeal. An archivist digging through the files had discovered a collection of fascinating links between the hospital and the Royal Family since Queen Victoria became its patron in 1852. At that time, 21,000 children under the age of ten died in London every year, almost half the total deaths in the capital.

The gift was by way of an invitation for the Prince and Princess both to become patrons of the appeal; it was the idea of professional fund-raiser Marion Allford, who had been brought in as the appeal director. No male member of the Royal Family had ever been directly involved with the hospital before, but she feels strongly that when children are in hospital it is the parents' problem, not just the mother's, and so the request was specifically for them both to be patrons.

They agreed, although they made it clear that they were not prepared to involve William or Harry in the exercise. So in October 1987 the Wishing Well Appeal was officially launched by the Prince, via satellite link from Highgrove. He was particularly pleased to be patron of Great Ormond Street, he said, because he had been there himself as a child. On one occasion doctors had come to Buckingham Palace to take his tonsils out, but on the other occasion he had been what he called, 'a blue light special'; he was rushed to the hospital with acute appendicitis, where the nurses, he said, had spoilt him rotten. Named after the fountain that originally stood in the

Diana greets Father Christmas outside Great Ormond Street Children's Hospital before delivering the presents

Diana always makes an effort to talk to children at their level

hospital garden, where children threw coins to wish for good health, the Wishing Well Appeal became one of the most successful fund-raising campaigns ever conducted. In well under the two years they had allowed themselves, the appeal had a total of £54 million with a further £30 million promised by the government. In a fifteen-month period either Charles and Diana, or both, had attended eleven special events for the appeal, and held several private receptions in addition.

They had hosted a cocktail party at Kensington Palace, for example, for the heads of all the major national clubs and associations with large memberships; these habitually adopt a charity to support each year. The Prince made a short speech about the needs of the hospital, and then both he and Diana went round the room and spoke to everyone individually, with the result that the Wishing Well Appeal spread like wildfire. The emotive logo – the crudely drawn child's face with a big blue teardrop rolling from its eye – became familiar to every family in Britain. Donations were pouring into the appeals office in the basement of Great Ormond Street at the rate of £2 million a month. So fast, in fact, that they had to call a halt to it.

But December was a day for the children. Diana waited outside the main entrance of Great Ormond Street holding a clutch of excited little hands for a good five minutes before the Wishing Well song, which pop star Boy George had specially recorded for the appeal, struck up; and then Father Christmas, in the shape of a heavily disguised Jimmy Tarbuck, juddered round the corner on his sleigh, pulled by two little white ponies. The sleigh was piled high with presents donated by the Variety Club, which he and the Princess then took into the hospital and distributed to the children inside.

It was the Princess at her best; completely natural and giving each child her undivided attention. When she is doing anything with children, she always squats down to their level, touches them and listens to them, and the response she gets in just a few moments with each is quite extraordinary.

Having delivered the presents, however, her next stop was the basement, which had been hastily and frugally fitted out to house the appeals office, with its six telephone lines and fifty cramped volunteers drafted in to handle the money as it flooded in. It was very basic indeed, and only by dint of preparation for the royal visitor did it have any carpeting on the stairs. Yet the volunteers had been beavering away down there for two months, working well into the night on many occasions, and were to be there for many more months to come. They were the unsung heroes of the whole appeal. Diana had said she would look in to say hello to give them a morale boost, but when one of her staff saw the route she had to take to get there they said she could not possibly go. It was positively hazardous. The only access to the basement was down a flight of steep steps, and involved ducking under a low ceiling. 'Nonsense,' said the Princess, and set off down the stairs at a spanking pace.

Diana has grown increasingly fit over the years. Like the Prince, she takes a great deal of exercise, and frequently leaves the people who escort her on visits around the country struggling to keep up. She is also hugely inquisitive, and unless they have planned their route carefully, and can keep safely abreast of her, Diana is quite likely to open interesting-looking doors to see what is behind them. Something else the organizers have learned is that the Princess will never skip a bed in a hospital ward, or a group of people in a room.

The Royal Marsden Hospital, the country's leading cancer hospital, discovered this very early on. If Diana has to walk through a ward with twenty beds in it, she will stop and talk to the occupant of each and every one, and the timekeepers just have to get ulcers. It is far better, they have realized, to limit the tour.

The Prince is rather easier to keep tabs on, but there is always the unforeseen to disrupt even the best-laid plans. Just last summer he was visiting Fort Perbrook, in Portsmouth, built in Napoleonic times, where an excellent youth-training

Diana laying the foundation stone for the new Royal Marsden Cancer hospital in Fulham, London

scheme was being run and he was to address a seminar. The Fort was a warren of underground tunnels and batteries and in every way a security nightmare, and the Prince's staff and members of BitC (also involved in the outing), who had done the recce, realized they had to get the Prince away from the youth schemes and down into the safety of the seminar very quickly.

As the helicopter came down to land, to their dismay they saw that the organizers had not only laid on about fifteen different activities for the Prince to inspect, including mountain-bike scrambling; but children from no fewer than five primary schools were gathered together in great banks to greet him. In thirty-eight minutes flat he was supposed to be addressing a very high-powered seminar on enterprise. The Prince became fascinated and vanished from sight into the mountain bikes, and it was twenty-four minutes before anyone could extract him and move him on.

Visiting a school in Doncaster in December 1989, Charles was on another very tight schedule, again with BitC. He had exactly eight minutes to hear a report back from business leaders who had been looking at inner-city schools. As the royal party came through the school gates, however, an entire youth brass orchestra, who again had obviously been at the ready for several hours on a cold wintry day, burst into life in the playground. The Prince, of course, had to go and say hello, and disappeared once again, emerging ten minutes later having had a long discussion with the chief brass player.

Many of Charles's ideas sprang from a memorable visit to Boston in September 1986, when he had been invited to speak at the Harvard 350th Commemoration Ceremony. It was an opportunity to talk about education and America, an irresistible combination as far as he was concerned, for which he happily interrupted his holiday at Balmoral. There was no pool of academics or professionals contributing to this talk; it was a speech very much from the heart, and the thoughts expressed – mocked by the tabloids, needless to say, as philosophical ramblings – are still very relevant today.

'I have heard a great deal about Harvard – who hasn't? After all, it has produced a cornucopia of leaders for the United States in many fields, not to mention the fact that six Harvard men have become President of the United States. I have also heard of Yale . . .

'I confess that I have not addressed such a large gathering since I spoke to 40,000 Gujerati buffalo farmers in India in 1980, and that was a rare experience.'

He moved on to the 'enduring significance and value of the Anglo-American relationship'.

'We must beware lest unscrupulous people exploit these areas of misunderstanding and divert our attention from the really important task, which is our common defence of the kind of freedoms we hold so dear: the freedoms for which this noble university so proudly stands and for which so many of its sons gave their lives in foreign fields.'

'Perhaps, too, as parents you may be wondering, like I do frequently, whether the educational system you are confronted with is the right one to produce the kind of balanced, tolerant, civilized citizens we all hope our children can become?'

The next day the Prince was leading a small group of businessmen he had brought over from Britain, including Stephen O'Brien, to look at a scheme called the Boston Compact, evidence that the United States had woken up sooner than anyone else to the dilemma of falling educational standards. It was a simple enough idea. Businesses in a central location are, more often than not, short of labour. Very often there are schools, just across the road, full of children who will very probably become unemployed when they leave because they will not be equipped to fill any of the jobs that are available. So, the businessman goes across the road to the people running the schools, and says, 'These are the jobs we want filled, if you can teach the children these skills we will give them priority if they come to us for a job when they leave.'

The Prince wanted BitC to try the same idea in Britain. So, in due course, a pilot Compact, or Education Partnership, was launched in the East End of London, linking four schools with eighteen local businesses.

There are now over forty Compacts in operation, which are succeeding – as much as anything by involving parents in the deal. It has been working miracles. Parents who previously took no interest in their children's education have suddenly become motivated. In London, the Compact has been so successful that children who would previously have left as soon as they reached the school-leaving age of sixteen, are deciding to stay on at school to take further exams. The companies who thought they were buying themselves employees to stack their shelves or deliver mail are getting nothing of the sort. They are all rather proud of the outcome; and the Prince is delighted.

The Prince now has a strong team behind him, which is more in tune with his activities than ever before, and better qualified. Sir John Riddell went back to the City, and was replaced by Major General Sir Christopher Airy, recently retired from commanding the Household Division, admirable qualifications for the job. The Prince also has three assistant private secretaries – Peter Westmacott, who is on secondment from the Foreign Office, and advises on diplomatic niceties; Commander Richard Aylard, retired from the Navy, who is Comptroller of the Household, and the Prince's resident environmental expert; and Guy Salter, with business expertise. It is a stronger team than the Prince has had before, but still understaffed, given that, as well as finding material for his speeches and meetings, they also have to research and organize his day trips and foreign tours, liaise with the press office and the Princess's assistant private secretary, Patrick Jephson, over their diaries, as well as handle the colossal amount of mail that arrives by every post. It is a punishing job, and Charles is no easy man to work for. He is a perfectionist, and he is impatient. Yet, at the same time, he inspires extraordinary loyalty.

15

Tragedy in the Snow

On a sunny afternoon in March 1988 the laughter went out of both of their lives. They were in Klosters again on their annual skiing holiday, later than usual because of the Australian bicentennial celebrations, but as always they were staying with the Palmer-Tomkinsons. Also in the party was the Duchess of York, alone because the Duke was at sea, and another close friend, thirty-five-year-old Major Hugh Lindsay, an equerry to the Queen, and an accomplished skier. He was also on his own. His wife Sarah, whom he had been married to for barely eight months, was pregnant, and had stayed at home in London, where she worked in the press office at Buckingham Palace.

As usual, Charles and Diana obliged the cameras with the first-day photocall, and were then left to get on with their holiday. It was looking good, the sky was blue and the snow conditions were perfect. Within hours, though, tragedy had struck. Hugh Lindsay lay dead beneath a wall of snow and Patti Palmer-Tomkinson, revived by mouth-to-mouth resuscitation, lay seriously injured.

They were skiing off-piste in deep virgin snow off the beaten track, one of the most exciting experiences on skis, full of uncertainty and undoubtedly more dangerous than skiing on the recognized runs. Suddenly, 'with a tremendous roaring', an avalanche was upon them. The rest of the group – Prince Charles, Patti's husband Charles, an alpine guide called Bruno Sprecher, and a Swiss policeman – were all spared by a whisker, and watched with horror as their two friends were swept clean away, engulfed in tons of snow as it hurtled on down the mountain.

Fortunately, the skiers were all wearing radio-detection devices, so they managed to find both bodies quite quickly. Bruno Sprecher took charge. He found Patti Palmer-Tomkinson first and gave her the kiss of life, then left the Prince to dig her out of the snow while he went in search of Hugh Lindsay. His body was buried higher up, but there was no chance of reviving him; he had died instantly.

In the chaos of the next hour, as reports of an accident seeped through to London, where Sarah Lindsay, still known by her maiden name of Sarah Brennan, happened to be on duty in the Buckingham Palace press office, there were stories that the Prince was in hospital and that the Princess and the Duchess of York were missing. The two women were in fact safely at home in the chalet, unaware of the drama on the moun-

In Klosters again, before tragedy struck

A sad day. Bringing their friend Hugh Lindsay's body home to RAF Northolt

tainside. Fergie had had a fall during the morning and, being three months pregnant, had decided to take the afternoon off. Diana had stayed with her.

The next twenty-four hours were probably the worst the Prince had ever been through. He was openly weeping as he travelled in the helicopter that brought the bodies down the mountain. Hugh Lindsay – young, tough, fit and full of enthusiasm for life one minute, with a new wife, excited about a baby on the way – was suddenly dead, in just seconds. Patti Palmer-Tomkinson, active and vibrant, was alive, but only just; her legs were badly crushed and it was doubtful whether she would ever walk again. It was only by the grace of God that the rest of them were safe. They were all profoundly shocked, filled with grief and remorse and uncertainty about why it had happened, and whether they were to blame in any way.

The next day Charles, Diana and Fergie flew home to RAF Northolt, bringing with them the body of their friend. His widow, Sarah, six months pregnant, was waiting to meet them. It was a sad, sad day, an unenviable reunion.

An inquiry determined that the skiers had probably precipitated the avalanche themselves, and questions raged in the press about the rights and wrongs of off-piste skiing – and whether Charles had coerced the others into taking risks that afternoon and whether he was ultimately responsible. Also, was it right for the heir to the throne to be risking his life in this way?

Charles may not have found it easy to sleep at night, but he was not responsible for the accident. Each of the skiers in that party had known the dangers they were courting when they set off that afternoon. They were all good, experienced skiers, who enjoyed what the Prince called the 'special dimension' of off-piste skiing and knew the risks it involved. Avalanches can happen to anyone, anywhere, at any time; they are a fact of life that anyone who skis knows about, whether they are beginners or experts. They are, as Charles himself said, 'a natural phenomenon of the mountains, and when it comes to avoiding them no one is infallible'. An avalanche two days later that killed people as they slept in their beds at Davos was proof of that. Nevertheless, the entire episode weighed heavily on the Prince. He flew out to Klosters several times in the following weeks and months to visit Patti Palmer-Tomkinson in hospital, and both he and Diana kept closely in touch with Sarah Lindsay.

It was a difficult period for Diana too. It was the first time she had witnessed such raw and naked grief; it was also her first experience of the death of someone close. And there was the awesome realization that her husband had very nearly been killed too. She grew up a lot that day. The next hurdle for them all was the funeral, held at the Memorial Chapel at Sandhurst. Ten members of the Royal Family were there – more than there had been at any funeral service since the Duke of Windsor's two years before – and a thousand friends, relatives, fellow officers and men from the 9th/12th Royal Lancers. Charles read the lesson.

He then sought refuge in the Highlands. Diana meanwhile stayed at home with the children and put a brave face on it. Even the day before the funeral she had insisted upon keeping to her work schedule, and no one would have guessed the torment she was suffering. It was a Birthright visit to a fitness centre in Holywell, near Clwyd in North Wales, where a whole array of little girls dressed up as characters from nursery rhymes awaited her. There were no grand people to meet, just some spiders and Little Miss Muffets, all of whom had been busily practising their curtsies and their 'Ma'ams' for weeks, and Diana did not let them down.

The Princess only cancels engagements when there is no option. Both she and the Prince are painfully aware that every engagement represents a gathering of people for whom this is a big day. They have prepared and rehearsed, possibly gone out and bought new clothes, and had their hair done for the occasion; they may even have redecorated the building in the Prince or Princess's honour, and have looked forward to this as a day they will remember and talk about for the rest of their lives. They both feel very strongly that these people should not be disappointed, and that there should be no hitches in the arrangements, no embarrassments.

One of the rare occasions when Diana did cancel, was in May 1988 when Prince Harry was rushed into Great Ormond Street Hospital for an emergency hernia operation. Like his father, he was 'a blue light special', and Diana had spent the night with him at the hospital. The following evening she was supposed to have attended a Mother and Child exhibition in aid of Birthright, but Anne Beckwith-Smith telephoned a couple of hours beforehand to say the Princess was so exhausted that she could not make it. While she had been in the hospital, she had not hidden herself away in Harry's room; she had gone out into other wards, while her son was under the anaesthetic, to talk to other sick children and their parents. It had been a draining twenty-four hours.

Despite Earl Spencer's curious plea for her to spend more time at home being a mother, Diana has always been the central figure in William and Harry's lives. She has always tried to work her schedule around them, and has very much been a warm and close mother to them. Unless she has to be in the north of England or even further afield, she will take them to school in the mornings, before going back to Kensington Palace to change for the day's engagements. On the whole, nothing is scheduled to go on much later than 3.30 in the afternoon, so that she can be back home again in time for their tea and bath before bed. Frequently, though, like the

Prince, she spends longer with people than has been allowed for, so schedules usually run a little late. On her way home she often pops into her local branch of Sainsbury's to buy the boys some Twiglets or some other treat that they particularly like. 'I know they're not very good for them,' she will say, 'but they do love them.'

On Friday afternoons they invariably set off for the country. Diana usually drives the boys, and the nanny follows with all the gear. Charles seldom manages to get away as early as Diana, and often drives down later. At Highgrove the children have far greater freedom than in London, and they love the countryside. They can roam about the garden and farm and see all the animals. There is a climbing frame on the lawn and a swing, there's the swimming pool, and their tree-house, and plenty of hedges for all sorts of games. They have their hamsters there, which live up in the nursery on the top floor of the house, and the Prince's two Jack Russells, Tigger – a present from Lady Salisbury in 1986 – and her daughter Roo, who generally stay at Highgrove unless the family is going to be away for longer than a week. They have ponies at Highgrove too. Both boys are very keen riders, and go off to local gymkhanas and shows in the summer. They have practice jumps in the fields, and a riding instructor comes to give them lessons. When they spend holidays at Sandringham or Balmoral, the ponies go too.

If Charles is at home, the boys often garden with him, or go for a drive or a walk round the farm. Charles and Diana both firmly believe in teaching their children good manners. It has been a struggle – they are no different from any other young boys – but they are both impeccably behaved nowadays, at least when on parade. King Constantine, who is Prince William's godfather, says that Charles treats them like young adults. He does not force them to do anything, but explains and reasons with them. William, whom he usually refers to as Wombat, is bright, exhausting and extremely wilful, and would stretch even the patience of a saint at times. One day, when he was four, he went with his father to the farm. It was a freezing cold day and William had no gloves. As his hands became colder he began to grumble, and finally he started to cry. 'I told you to bring some gloves,' said Charles, 'and you wouldn't listen, so shut up.'

Diana is no stranger to supermarkets!

Diana arranges her schedule so she can take the boys to school most days

He used to run rings around his mother too. Stephen O'Brien and Cathy Ashton were sitting in the Prince's study at Kensington Palace waiting for the Prince to arrive for a meeting one evening, when Diana burst through the door, clearly not expecting to find anyone so large inside. 'I'm sorry,' she said, 'I'm looking for William. It's bedtime so he's vanished. Will you give me a shout if you see him?' Cathy Ashton was left quietly wondering how one might give the Princess of Wales a shout, when giggles from above indicated that it would not be necessary.

Another visitor to encounter the boys in full cry was Roger Singleton, director of Barnardo's. He arrived at Kensington Palace for lunch one day, bearing a large plaster frog. The frog was a gift from some physically handicapped children at a school in Taunton which Diana had visited the previous week. The children were being taught simple trades, including filling moulds with plaster of Paris, and painting the resulting object. Diana had been asked if she would like a frog. 'I'd love one,' she said and, since Roger happened to be seeing her the next week, he had undertaken to deliver it.

The butler opened the front door and, as Roger was carrying this great green horror along the corridor, William and Harry came bouncing down the stairs and started clamouring to have the frog. It was too heavy for either of them to carry, so William went racing off up the stairs, excitedly telling his mother that a frog was coming.

Harry refused to be parted from it, so he and Roger shared it, and, with one small hand supporting the frog's bottom and the other firmly clasping Roger's hand to help him up the stairs, the trio progressed slowly upwards, to be met at the top by Diana, who had come to see what all the fuss was about.

She is a good instinctive mother, clearly besotted by her sons, and determined to ensure that they grow up into secure adults. How this is achieved is something Diana has become increasingly interested in, not only in her work with Barnardo's, but also with Relate.

Relate, previously called the Marriage Guidance Council, had first written to the Princess in 1987, asking whether she would consider becoming patron of their Golden Jubilee Appeal in 1988, when they hoped to raise £1 million. The charity has been the largest provider of counselling to married couples since it was founded in 1938; they counsel over 50,000 clients a year, but felt that it was time to bring it more up to date. Society's needs are changing and problems go far beyond the partners in a marriage, so the charity felt they should be reflecting that. Thus, to coincide with their Golden Jubilee, they planned to relaunch under the new name, with a wider range of services more appropriate to the needs of the 1990s. 'Relate helps people who need to talk to someone about marriage and relationships – relationships with partners, with children, with parents, at home or at work.'

The Princess, came the reply, was too heavily committed to take on another patronage, but she would be very interested to see the work they did; so, in March 1988, not long after Hugh Lindsay's funeral, Diana went to Rugby to visit their

Charles treats his sons like young adults. A 40th birthday photograph taken at Highgrove

national headquarters. She was there for one and a quarter hours and, as well as hearing about the work they did such as counselling, sex therapy, education and training, she also watched a role-playing session. It was a classic situation, which they use in their counsellor-training programmes, where a counsellor had to deal with a couple, played by experienced trainers, who were in the midst of a fierce marital row. It was very real and very powerful, and Diana was riveted. She immediately asked to see more, so six weeks later she went to visit a neighbourhood centre in London. She was clearly very interested in the work they did. From the start she was asking acute and sensitive questions about what makes a good marriage, and a recurrent interest has been what effect the quality of a marriage can have on the children.

According to Relate's figures, there are over 151,000 divorces in Britain a year – that is, two marriages in five break down, and that gives this country the highest divorce rate in Europe. Those figures involve 149,000 children under the age of sixteen; one third of those children are under five, and more than two thirds are between five and ten; and there is evidence that such children are very seriously affected by the break-up of the family unit. Dramatic research published recently has shown that the delinquency rate in children whose parents divorced when the offspring were between the ages of five and twenty-one is twice as high as for those children whose parents remained together. There is increasing awareness of the damaging effect of divorce, and much of the work that Relate now does involves children, and giving them the support that their parents are very often unable to give them when their own lives are in turmoil. Having experienced her own parents' divorce when she was six years old, this is an area in which Diana is especially interested.

She opened a pilot centre in Portsmouth in 1989, set up specifically to deal with whole families, to help them sort out the difficulties of adjusting to one another; and, where a marriage is coming to an end, to help limit the damage inflicted on the children by a messy divorce. On that occasion she listened to the problems of a couple who were living together, who had both been married before, and both had three children from their previous marriages. All eight of them were endeavouring to live under one roof and had discovered that it was not as simple as it seemed. The whole situation was fraught with difficulty: not just for the adults, but for the children who were suddenly thrown together with complete strangers, given a new parent and, understandably, had very mixed emotions.

Over the years the Princess has listened in on, and participated in, many counselling sessions, dealing with all manner of problems – those of single mothers, the elderly, mixed-culture marriages, and couples with sexual problems. The clients have simply been asked whether they would mind having an observer in the room, and have been astonished to find that that observer was the Princess of Wales, and that after a while they were confiding in her as though she were another professional.

'She is very gifted,' says director David French. 'She forms relationships with people very quickly. It's a real skill; she is acutely sensitive and attuned to atmosphere, and knows how to cope with it. Clients come out saying "She really got us talking".'

Such was the regularity with which she continued to visit that David French asked once again whether she would become patron of Relate, and in April 1989 she agreed.

'Despite all the change around us,' she said soon afterwards, 'the family remains the bedrock upon which modern society is built. Relate is working to help families: to help couples and, thereby, to help the children who are so often the victims of marriage breakdown.'

The effect was to give the whole business of marriage guidance, which still has something of a stigma attached to it, a tremendous boost. Throughout its history the organization has had to fight prejudice. It was started by a seventy-year-old clergyman, who simply intended to research the problems of marriage and divorce; but he was so swamped by requests for help from couples that counselling became its mainstay. But there were people who disapproved. As late as the 1950s, the *Daily Sketch* was calling it 'a group of busybodies whose language, put a little more crudely, would lead them into the dock for indecency'. Having the Princess of Wales, a young and glamorous mother, as patron made it far more acceptable to the public. And it is not just an important area for the individuals concerned; problems at home cost the country millions of pounds every year in absenteeism and underperformance. They are a prime cause of stress-related ailments, a major source of illness, and can also lead to family violence and crimes involving child abuse.

Since 1989 Diana has become increasingly involved in the mechanics of counselling. She has taken part in training sessions, where she has joined in on discussion groups involving real cases; every counsellor takes part in these once a fortnight. On one occasion, the Princess took the part of observer in a role-playing exercise, which is another essential tool of counsellor training. The observer sits in on a session between a counsellor and 'clients', just as Diana had done on her initial visit to Rugby; but as observer, her role is to comment on what is going on in the room between the three participants, and analyse the situation.

Every counsellor learns a tremendous amount about themselves in the process of helping others. They get valuable insight into human nature and the ingredients that go to make and break relationships; they thus develop a deeper understanding and tolerance, which inevitably helps to strengthen their own marriages. Diana is obviously not a counsellor – it takes two years to train – but she has been a very willing pupil, and has learnt a lot during her time with Relate about people's needs, fears and insecurities, and about the importance, above all else, of communication. She has seen how essential it is that people take a realistic view of themselves and their situation, and recognize the effect that their attitudes and behaviour have on those around them, especially their families. She has seen the damage that can be inflicted on children; and there is no doubt that Diana has put everything she has learnt into helping solve the problems within her own marriage.

Diana's Appetite

There has been monotonous speculation on and off for the last ten years that the Princess of Wales suffers from the slimmers' disease anorexia nervosa. It was first mentioned before the wedding, when she lost more than a stone, and was still very much the talk among reporters on their tour of Wales after the honeymoon. If she was, they said, might it not decrease her fertility? The announcement two weeks later that she was pregnant put paid to that line of speculation for a while; but soon after William's birth she once again lost a dramatic amount of weight, and the question of anorexia was resurrected.

Of all the myths that have grown up nothing has caused Diana more amusement. She has always had a very healthy appetite. Even as a teenager, while her fellow dance students at Miss Vacani's would sip slimming cups of Bovril for their lunch, Diana would cross the road to the Express Dairy opposite and tuck into chicken pieces and real food. The weight she lost initially was partly planned, but mostly a result of the stress she was under in the lead-up to the wedding. After William's birth the weight simply fell off her, as it does for many women when they have babies, particularly if they are breast-feeding, as Diana was. Nowadays her weight is virtually stable. She eats healthily, a lot of salads and vegetables from the garden at Highgrove, but still quite heartily. She takes so much exercise nowadays, though, that she would be unlikely to put on any weight no matter what she ate.

The myth has been fuelled by receptions where people see her pushing a tomato or a piece of lettuce round a plate and eating next to nothing. This is because she finds it very hard to hold a plate, talk and eat at the same time, and maintain any semblance of dignity. Buffet meals are a nightmare, and nowadays she has learnt to eat beforehand. The schedule usually states that the Princess is taking ten minutes for a briefing or to powder her nose, and during that time she will have a quick plate of sandwiches. The result is that people have come away from these occasions saying 'She didn't eat a thing', and the anorexia theory has gained credence.

At sit-down dinners it is another matter entirely. John Young was organizing a gala dinner for the National Hospital at the Goldsmith's Hall in September 1988, and had asked Diana what she would like to eat. She chose soup followed by saddle of lamb. Arriving early for the dinner to check that everything was in order, he went

The Sultan of Oman gave Diana a dazzling diamond
and sapphire set of necklace, earrings and bracelet

*Anorexic? No myth has amused Diana more.
In Sydney, nine months after the birth of William*

into the kitchen to find his chef, Mr Smith, in a state of total panic. 'You've made the most dreadful mistake,' he said. How could he possibly serve saddle of lamb to the Princess? Didn't Mr John, as he is known in the family brewery business, know she was a vegetarian and anorexic to boot? Ask any of the waitresses, they knew.

Mr John became a little uneasy, but insisted that Diana had specifically chosen the lamb; if he were wrong, he would bear the consequences. 'Well, the Princess gobbled up the first two courses,' he recalls with a certain amount of merriment. 'There were four or five cutlets on her plate and she ate the lot, and picked up the bones and ate them with her fingers. I left one because I couldn't eat any more, and she looked at my plate and said:

' "Aren't you going to eat that? It's frightfully rude to leave it."

' "No", I said, "I was always taught by my mother to leave something on my plate for Mr Manners."

'Then we had lemon soufflé for pudding and she asked whether she could have a second helping!'

As her weight has fluctuated over the years, going up with pregnancy and then dramatically down, her clothes have needed to be altered, and also her jewellery. David Thomas has enlarged her pearl chokers when she has been pregnant, and also her engagement ring, to accommodate her swollen fingers.

David Thomas had been at Collingwoods, where the Spencer family had bought their jewellery and silverware, for twenty-six years. Charles had bought her engagement ring from Garrard's – at a cost of £28,500 – which, as the Crown Jewellers, he had always used. But Charles subsequently fell out with Garrard's and Diana introduced him to David Thomas.

The introduction was somewhat nerve-racking. It was in April 1981, while Charles and Diana were still engaged. The Prince had just returned from Australia, where he had broken his little finger playing polo, and David was summoned to Buckingham Palace to cut his signet ring off. The finger was badly swollen and the ring was deeply imbedded. It was a very difficult operation, and David was terrified he was going to cut the Prince.

'Will you send me to the Tower if I cut your finger off?' he asked tentatively.

'Yes,' said the Prince.

'Don't worry,' said Diana, 'I'll come and visit you.'

From that day onwards David Thomas looked after the Prince as well as the Princess, much to Garrard's distress. So in 1986 Garrard's wooed David Thomas with a directorship, to entice him to move to their great emporium in Regent Street. He was sorely tempted, but wanted to consult the Prince and Princess first. So he telephoned Charles and asked whether he could drop into Highgrove on his way back from Wales one weekend and talk to him. As a result of their conversation the Prince said he was only too pleased to move with him to Garrard's. While they talked in the house, Diana took his wife around the garden.

So it has been David Thomas over the years who has looked after all of Diana's jewellery. He cleans and restores it, and keeps the important pieces locked away in a safe at Garrard's, bringing them out when the Princess wants them – for state occasions, for example, when he will deliver them to Kensington Palace. She has some very valuable items among the collection, some old, some new. The Queen has given her several pieces, most of which belonged to Queen Mary, including a sturdy diamond and pearl tiara, and an emerald and diamond choker, which Diana attached to a piece of ribbon and wore as a headband for a ball in Melbourne in 1985. She did this again in Japan the following year, with diamonds and sapphires that had originally been set in a watch that was part of a fabulous set – given to her by the Saudi Arabian Royal Family as a wedding present. More priceless gifts have come from foreign tours, especially to the Middle East. The Sultan of Oman gave her a dazzling diamond and sapphire set of necklace, earrings and bracelet, during their 1986 visit. Another important piece is a seven-strand pearl choker with a huge sapphire clasp; also, a solid amethyst and diamond cross, that sits on a long rope of pearls, and a diamond necklace with a pendant of the Prince of Wales feathers – an engagement present from the Queen Mother.

The three-strand pearl choker that she wore so much in the early years, she bought for herself before she became engaged. The simple gold D that she also used to wear a lot, and still resurrects on occasions, was a present that her friends at school had clubbed together to give her for her birthday one year. The Prince has given her jewellery too. He gave her an antique emerald and diamond bracelet as a wedding present, a gold and pearl heart-shaped necklet when Prince William was born, and a gold charm bracelet, to which he regularly adds new charms.

Diana has always loved jewellery, but she has recently become very interested in the history of the jewels she has, and David Thomas is currently cataloguing the pieces. He keeps a record of everything that she has been given on foreign trips, so that when the donor comes to Britain, or she goes there again, she can greet him wearing the right jewels. For fear of offending the donors, she has to be careful about adapting the jewels she has been given. Most items have simply been lengthened or shortened, but she has turned a lot of the sapphires and diamonds that the Saudis

She is more likely to buy fake jewellery for herself these days

gave her at the time of the wedding into a number of smaller pieces.

Not all presents, however, have been jewellery, and not all have been entirely to either the Prince or the Princess's taste. One of the gifts they brought home from the Gulf was a vast and priceless sculpture of a desert scene, intricately crafted in gold and silver, complete with date trees and amethyst dates hanging from them. It was boxed up and put smartly into the safe, until there was a sudden SOS call from the palace to say the donor of this particular piece was coming to dinner, and they needed it out and on display as quickly as possible.

Charles and Diana take presents for their hosts on foreign tours too, which as often as not come from Garrard's. These are paid for by the Foreign Office if it is an official visit but, unlike most other members of the Royal Family, the Prince takes a great interest in finding the right gift. He will ask for a selection of silver teasets, for example, to be sent round to his office in St James's Palace, and he will choose from those.

Garrard's is a favourite port of call. The Princess will frequently telephone from her car to say she is on her way and will be there two or three minutes later. She expects no ceremony, she comes in like any ordinary customer, and as often as not sits at one of the counters on the floor of the shop, rather than being taken into a private office. She comes to buy presents for friends, and occasionally pieces for herself too – although rarely these days. She is far more likely to buy fake costume jewellery for herself, much of which comes from the fashionable little shop Butler and Wilson in the Fulham Road. She is very generous in buying for others, as is the Prince, although she does not have limitless funds. She will quite often say, 'Oh no, that's far too expensive.' Nevertheless, when Anne Beckwith-Smith left her full-time staff last summer she gave her a pair of very special earrings.

Although 1988 had been marred in its early months by tragedy, the incident in many ways brought the Prince and Princess closer together. Diana was able to help Charles through his grief and pain in a way that she could not have done in the past. She had grown immeasurably: no longer wrapped up in herself, no longer overawed by the attention, no longer thrown by the media. She had found her métier, listening to people and their problems, and she understood that the Prince's grief would take time. She also understood that he needed time by himself. She had come to know the man she had married, come to realize that he had to be left to his own devices, to work things through for himself.

It was a significant year altogether: Diana made her first speech to the outside world, for Barnardo's; and Charles made his first film, which had enormous impact, not just in Britain, but all over the world. It was also the year of his fortieth birthday.

After his famous 'Luftwaffe' speech at the Mansion House, a BBC television producer called Christopher Martin approached the Prince with the idea of writing and presenting an hour-long programme about architecture. Charles was extremely dubious about the idea, but nevertheless intrigued. All his interventions on the subject in the past had been twenty-minute speeches, and television was a medium he knew nothing about. The potential for looking foolish was great. On the other hand, he did have a message he wanted to deliver and television was clearly the best means. After a great deal of deliberation he cautiously agreed.

So during the summer of 1988, the script was written and the various strands filmed in a number of locations in England, Scotland, Wales, America and Italy. It was a tortuous process, during which time the producer was no less nervous than the performer that it might all be a disaster; but by September, when Christopher Martin took the finished product up to Balmoral to show it to Charles, he was aware that he had an extraordinarily powerful film on his hands.

As they sat watching it in the ballroom, Christopher Martin mused upon his last visit to the castle. After leaving university in 1961 he had had a job as firelighter at Balmoral, and had toiled away below stairs, stoking the fires and the old kitchen ranges with coal and wood. His day had begun at 4.30 in the morning to ensure that the ovens were hot enough for the chefs to cook the royal breakfast.

'Oh, do you remember old so and so?' said Charles when he heard this. Alas, Christopher remembered none of the old boys who had worked there, but he did remember the Prince, aged twelve, coming into the kitchens to get a handful of carrots for the ponies. Little did he think, as he stood across the kitchen table from him, that he would be sitting with the Prince nearly thirty years later in the ballroom, having made a film that would become headline news all over the world.

The film appeared, entitled *A Vision of Britain*, and a book of the same name sold more than 200,000 copies. Once again, the Prince explained his feelings about modern architecture, and with the aid of the camera took his audience on a guided tour of all that he hated most.

In Birmingham he took us to the proposed new convention centre, the plans for which he had seen the year before. 'Choosing my words to be as inoffensive as possible, I said I thought it was an unmitigated disaster.

'Facing the fine Town Hall and Art Gallery, *this* was built. It's the central library – but how can you tell? It looks like a place where books are incinerated, not kept.

'Look at the Bull Ring. It's a planned accident.'

Moving on to London he said, 'Look at the National Theatre. It seems like a clever way of building a nuclear power station in the middle of London without anyone objecting.'

The new British Library: 'It has no character to suggest that it is a great public building. And is this really a reading room? It looks more like an assembly hall of an academy for secret police.

'It's not easy nowadays to remember how Wren's City churches used to surround the glorious dome of St Paul's like so many yachts riding at anchor around a great ship.

'The London that slowly evolved after the Great Fire took about three hundred years to build. It took about fifteen years to destroy.

'Our age is the first to have despised the principles of mathematical harmony and proportion and to have embarked on a course which glorifies man's domination over nature and the triumph of science.

'When did we lose our sense of vision?'

His critics lost no time in answering. The following week another programme gave the architects a chance to hit back, and several launched into print as well.

'The Prince might consider whether the charges of paternalism and unaccountability, with which he criticizes architects,' said a furious Richard Rogers, 'might not more aptly be directed towards his own way of doing things.

'In fact, the real sadness is that public discussion of architecture has been dominated by invective and vilification rather than informed debate.'

Maxwell Hutchinson was every bit as angry. 'Are we really saying that a Georgian town house is the apex of urban living? We might just as well argue for a return to the horse and cart . . . Decorating our cities with the reproduction furniture of neo-classicism is as absurd as repainting a Constable landscape with a Vauxhall Cavalier in the foreground.

'His [the Prince's] is the single most powerful voice in the architectural forum today. He is surfing into the 1990s on a high tide of public opinion.

'But the mandate for his views on architecture was deduced before it was proven. His views are simultaneously innocuous and destructive.'

17

The Organic Gardener

Whatever the mandate for his views on architecture, *A Vision of Britain* was a colossal success with ordinary people. Letters of support and thanks for articulating what they thought, but felt unqualified to say, flooded into St James's Palace and left Charles feeling better than he had done for a long time; he was confident as he approached his fortieth birthday that he was heading in the right direction. It was not just the architecture. All sorts of things were coming together. Life was looking up, and beginning to make some sort of sense.

The very day *A Vision of Britain* was broadcast, Friday, 28 October 1988, the Prince held a horticultural lunch at Highgrove, which he enjoyed enormously. It was a very informal gathering of eight people, among whom were the director of the National Fruit Trials at Brogdale; Lord Kitchener, chairman of the Henry Doubleday Research Association, the national centre for organic gardening; and Alan Gear, its chief executive.

Alan and his wife, Jackie, who is also his business partner, had been writing to the Prince on and off since 1983, when he delivered his message of support to the Cirencester organic food conference. They knew he was converting part of his farm to organic agriculture; they also knew he was a keen gardener, and thought he should therefore be gardening organically. So over the years they had sent him their periodic newsletter and an open invitation to visit the Association at Ryton Gardens near Coventry. In return, they had always had standard, polite letters thanking them, written on behalf of the Prince.

So Alan Gear thought it was a practical joke when, sitting at his desk one morning, the girl on the switchboard told him Buckingham Palace was on the line. 'Go on,' he said, and was about to put the phone down, when a voice that sounded very authentic said that the Prince of Wales wanted to hold a horticultural lunch at Highgrove, and would the Association like to send a couple of representatives.

A few weeks later Alan Gear was swinging through the gates at Highgrove and up the winding driveway with two bottles of organic burgundy on the back seat as a gift for his host.

First on the agenda was a conducted tour of the walled garden, where Alan came up with a few suggestions. The Prince wanted to know how to deal with the problem

he was having with the cabbage caterpillar, for instance; and he had never heard of biological control in the greenhouse, which Alan was able to explain.

By the time they sat down to lunch the two had built up a considerable rapport, and continued to talk about every topic from politics to fox hunting, including the importance of turning forty. The Prince's fortieth birthday was looming in just over two weeks; Alan's was in another six months. The lunch was entirely home produced and had had minimum preparation: beef, and seven varieties of vegetable that had been scrubbed rather than peeled. By the end of lunch he had promised to send the Prince all sorts of things including some Chinese vegetable seeds, some bacillus thuringiensis to kill off his cabbage caterpillars, and a catalogue of everything they sold. The Prince, in turn, had promised to become patron of the Henry Doubleday Research Association, and everyone else who had been sitting round the table wondered why they had come.

A month later the telephone rang again. It was the Prince's assistant private secretary, David Wright.

'Patronage brings duties as well as benefits, Mr Gear,' he said. 'The Prince has to deliver a speech to the Worshipful Company of Fruiterers. Can you write it for him please?'

'No' said Alan in horror, but as soon as he had confessed to his wife Jackie that he had said no, she told him to get straight back on the phone and say he had changed his mind. Dutifully he did this, and what he wrote formed the basis for a speech delivered the following February; this, once again, brought the Prince into confrontation with the government.

It involved Brogdale, the home of the National Fruit Trials near Faversham in Kent, which the government planned to close as part of cuts of £30 million from the horticultural research budget. Brogdale had been set up by the Ministry of Agriculture in 1916 to test fruit varieties for commercial growers, and housed over 2,000 different varieties of apples, 500 cultivars of pear and 350 different sorts of plums, as well as a wealth of other fruits. Its value is as a gene bank. Because the growers have been cutting down on the number of varieties they produce, the old strains have disappeared; and if they are not kept going somewhere, such as at Brogdale, they will die out.

Charles treated his hosts to some tales from abroad, and a quick dig at his critics:

I have come to the conclusion that it doesn't really matter what I say any more. I suspect this evening I may easily end up being accused of abusing my position unfairly and undemocratically to grow organic bananas on royal manure or some such unlikely activity.

My secondary role in life is as a food research scientist. Visiting the Arctic, where the Eskimos reside . . . I went round a school, where they were learning how to cut up and dissect a seal. There on the classroom floor was a dead seal neatly cut from knave to chaps and spread open on the floor. There was a very

Diana presenting Charles with a prize at the end of the charity polo match for the National Hospital

peculiar pong in the classroom, as you can imagine. To my absolute horror, a child suddenly appeared with a plate, and on it was cut up the seal's liver into little cubes and I was offered this thing.

I thought to myself, obviously I have to do this for England, so I took the bit of raw seal's liver and put it in my mouth. Now the trouble is what do you do, do you chew it? Or do you swallow it? If you chew it, it tastes like the smell of the dead seal that is lying on the floor and if you swallow it at once, it is very difficult to actually get your epiglottis to open sufficiently far enough to swallow this thing. Anyway I finally managed to swallow it without actually being sick, whereupon I turned to say to all the people who were with me, my staff and other people that it was their turn – they'd gone, all of them. The doctor who was attached to my staff said you might have got botulism as a result of eating that, I said thank you very much for telling me now.

His hosts at Plaisterers' Hall that night had provided all the fruit trees at Highgrove, 'one of the best wedding presents anybody ever gave us', he said.

'I bottle the plums that I grow from some of your trees, and every day for breakfast I eat them during the winter and when they are finished I start eating the rhubarb which you didn't give me that I grow in forcing pots in another part of the garden.

'Ladies and Gentleman, as I said, my garden gives me enormous pleasure and an endless source of conversation with various plants that inhabit it.'

Diana's interest in horticulture has always been strictly limited. She loves walking round the garden, and loves the house being full of flowers from it, particularly scented flowers. She knows what is what in the garden, and is very keen to show off the Prince's handiwork, but, as for doing any planting, digging or weeding, she does not want to know. Her weeding days were over long ago. When she was at school at West Heath, weeding was a punishment for minor misdemeanours. Ruth Rudge, the headmistress, used to make anyone caught talking after lights out, running in the corridors, or secreting chocolate bars in the dormitories, weed the garden and, although Diana may never have been keen, she was a practised hand all the same.

One of the areas, however, where she and Charles do coincide more often these days is at polo matches. Now that the boys are older and becoming interested in the game, especially William, Diana takes them to watch their father. Those are the occasions when the public sees her the way she dresses in private, in jeans and jumper, unostentatious and relaxed. She is well aware, however, that she is on show, even off duty, and enjoys being able to manipulate the press. At a match in 1988 she wore a British Lung Foundation sweatshirt, with the distinctive red balloon on it, and, putting her hand obligingly in her pocket as she walked past photographers so they had a good shot of the balloon, ensured that the charity had front-page exposure in the national press the following morning.

Diana had become patron of the British Lung Foundation at the beginning of 1986. It was a brand-new national charity, set up to raise money for research into

Diana, wearing a British Lung Foundation sweatshirt, at a polo match with William

lung disease, a common condition, about which very little was known, and very little money being put into finding out more. Less than 1 per cent of government and charity funds devoted to medical research goes into lung disease, yet it is the second most common cause of death in Britain. It affects between 5 and 10 per cent of the population – that is, over five million people – and not just the elderly, or the smoking population. Lung disease is thought to be one of the causes of 'cot death' in babies; it is the most common illness in children and the most frequent cause of their admission to hospital. Two or three children in every primary-school class suffer from some form of respiratory problem.

Without hesitation, Diana had agreed to become patron, and was immediately keen to learn about the lung; so on her first visit to the Brompton Hospital, chairman Dr Malcolm Green sat her down and gave her a short lecture with slides. She has had several more slide shows since, as she has gone about the country visiting hospitals where different areas of research are being carried out, and the lessons learnt have sunk in. At a reception for City businessmen in the Great Hall at St Bartholomew's Hospital in 1989, the Princess delivered a small lecture herself. In conversation with someone about allergic asthma, she said, 'It must be the house-dust mite,' and, when asked what that was, launched into a detailed and knowledgeable explanation of a tiny creature so small that twenty-five would fit on the head of a pin; the house-dust mite is the most frequent trigger for asthma attacks.

'Hey,' she said, suddenly aware that Malcolm Green was listening. 'I shouldn't be saying all this, you should.'

When asked to come to the reception, she had specifically asked that it be organized for National No Smoking Day, 8 March. Smoking is another subject on which Diana is capable of holding forth. Among the slides she was shown on that first visit to the Brompton were some horrifying pictures of smokers' lungs that had been eaten away by disease.

'If people could see pictures like that on television, they'd surely decide to give up smoking,' said the Princess. 'Can't you get them to show those on television?'

Smoking is a major cause of lung disease, and also lung cancer. It kills more men than any other sort of cancer, and the rate is increasing so fast in women that it will soon exceed breast cancer as the number-one killer. Between half and two thirds of smokers will die before they reach retirement age – and 'passive' smokers suffer too, particularly the children of smokers. They are more likely to have lung problems and are more frequently admitted to hospital as babies than the children of non-smokers.

It is a subject that Diana feels passionately about. She and Charles are both non-smokers; neither of them have ever smoked, and they do not approve of any of the people around them smoking. Nowadays if anyone asks whether she minds if they smoke in her presence, Diana says, 'You do realize that I am the patron of the British Lung Foundation.' 'That usually puts them off,' she says.

On her very first visit to the Brompton Hospital, she had been sitting on one sick child's bed when she noticed that his mother was holding a cigarette.

'What are you doing with that cigarette?' asked Diana, sharply.

'Nothing,' said the mother, who smoked forty a day.

'That's not true,' said the Princess. 'Please give it up.' It was said quite privately, and quite genuinely.

A more public endorsement of the anti-smoking campaign came in June 1990 when she opened a whole non-smoking wing at the Bath Spa Hotel, owned by Trusthouse Forte. The group had just announced a sponsorship deal with the British Lung Foundation, in which they were designating a third of the bedrooms in their 200 hotels as non-smoking rooms. That was a total of 6,000 rooms, which would each carry the British Lung Foundation balloon logo and have their literature in the room. The whole exercise not only earned the charity £100,000, but it will also ensure that the British Lung Foundation remains firmly in the public eye, as thousands of people a year pass through those rooms. The Trusthouse Forte group is not the only company to have designated non-smoking rooms. It is not pure sop to the anti-smoking lobby, it is sound economic sense. The furnishings in non-smoking rooms stay cleaner and last much longer than rooms in which people have smoked.

The Prince has never spoken publicly about smoking, and two of his personal private secretaries have smoked – Edward Adeane and Sir John Riddell smoked cigars – although not in his presence, and he never approved. He had been especially delighted, when dining with Spike Milligan one evening, to find a 'No Smoking' notice in the comedian's sitting-room. He was equally delighted by an excellent bottle of 1947 wine, which they shared, while reading aloud the verse of the appalling nineteenth-century Scots poet McGonagall, which the Prince had brought along.

Diana had not joined them. 'She's at home looking after the kids,' he had explained. A more plausible explanation could be that she had already heard McGonagall.

'You're the one that addresses my husband as Trainee King,' she said when they finally met. Diana, of course, was scarcely born at the time when the Prince was so addicted to the Goons.

Although the Prince and Princess spend a lot of time apart, they certainly take an interest in what the other is doing, and know who all the personalities are that they work with. Diana often greets people from BitC with accusations of being the ones who take up all of her husband's time. And during a period when Diana was working especially hard for Barnardo's, when she carried out three events in one week, culminating in a polo match, the Prince said to Roger Singleton, 'You see more of my wife than I do.'

Diana has regularly used polo matches to raise money for her charities. Birthright was one of the first to benefit in 1985. 'Oh Vivienne,' she said to Vivienne Parry, clasping Prince Charles, still hot and sweaty from the field, 'have you met my hubby?' The Barnardo's match was the following year, and in 1988 Diana nominated the National Hospital. That year the entire event was paid for by the Spanish magazine *Hello!*, which planned to launch in this country. They offered to sponsor a polo match for the Princess of Wales for the charity of her choice. It was the most extravagant affair. The Spanish owners of the magazine flew across 150 people from Spain for a spectacular lunch; they put up huge marquees at Smith's Lawn, with glittering chandeliers; planted orange trees specially flown over for the day; and at the end of it all the Princess was presented with a cheque for £35,000 for the National Hospital.

Diana has also raised money at tennis matches. Tennis is a game she has always loved. At school she would sit glued to the television throughout Wimbledon fortnight, and one of the perks she has enjoyed most as Princess of Wales has been the opportunity over the years to watch the world's most prestigious tennis tournament from the Royal Box. One of her favourite players is Pat Cash, and in June 1988 she attended an exhibition black-tie match between Pat Cash, Boris Becker, Stefan Edberg and Henri Leconte at the David Lloyd Centre. It was a mixture of serious tennis and showmanship, with Pat Cash throwing his famous head-bands into the audience. The Princess failed to catch one, but she had a wonderful evening, and £161,000 was raised that night for the Wishing Well Appeal. At the same time, she presented trophies to the people who had raised the most money in the London marathon in April, which had brought in a further £1,500,000 for the Appeal.

The Prince has never shown any interest in tennis, and although Diana said when she married him that as well as teaching him about ballet she would introduce him to tennis, she seems to have failed. She has managed to drag him along to pop concerts, however. He has never looked particularly comfortable at them, but he has certainly appreciated the money they have raised, especially for the Prince's Trust. The Michael Jackson concert at Wembley in July 1988, for example, shared between the Trust and the Wishing Well Appeal, raised £100,000 for each.

The Prince has become involved in a vast range of different ventures and concerns, but the Prince's Trust is still very dear to him. It was no coincidence that he chose to celebrate his fortieth birthday, with the attendant publicity, at a party in Birmingham, with 1,500 young people who had been helped by the Trust. It was held in an old tram depot in Aston, which unemployed trainees had restored and turned into a transport museum. Wearing a '40' badge on his lapel, he cut a huge three-tiered cake, specially made in his honour, and seemed as though he was in his element.

Charles has never shared Diana's enthusiasm for rock concerts; with Michael Jackson at the charity concert at Wembley, 1988

Turning Point

Up to the age of forty, the major influences in the Prince's life had been older men and women. The Queen Mother had played a vital role during childhood; Lord Mountbatten had seen him through adolescence and into manhood; there was Lord Butler at Cambridge; and George Thomas, now Lord Tonypandy, had guided him during the difficult period in Wales. There was also Sir Laurens van der Post, Sir Harold Acton, Sir Hugh Casson, and fellow Royal Academician John Ward, and Sir John Higgs at the Duchy. Lady Salisbury and Dr Miriam Rothschild also played their part. In addition, there was Harold Haywood at the Prince's Trust and Sir Ian Gourlay at United World Colleges. Dr Eric Anderson, his former English teacher at Gordonstoun, and now headmaster at Eton, was another influence. All these people, and more, had provided the source material from which the Prince drew inspiration and guidance.

Since turning forty, he has had a complete change in his life. He still respects the older generation and regards them as a source of immense wisdom, but the people he sees as vital now in the important work to be done in the community, in business, in architecture, in politics, and in saving the world, are his own generation: the age group that for most of his life he has virtually ignored.

He has worked with older people on behalf of younger people. As he has said time and again, 'young people are one of our country's most vital resources', and he is still dedicated to helping them realize their full potential; but it is the people in their late thirties and early forties that he has suddenly woken up to. It is people of this age all over the world to whom he wants to address himself and inspire and motivate, because he has come to realize that they are the ones who will rule the world for the next twenty years: they are powerful, bright and dynamic, they have the energy of youth, but the experience of age. They are a force for good in waiting, the key to success in every area he wants to tackle, and Charles finds them exciting company.

This has not only altered his outlook in his working life, but also at home. The yawning gap that there was in the early days between Charles and Diana, and their respective friends, has gradually grown smaller. They now have far more friends that they both enjoy being with: people like the Duke of Westminster and his wife Natalia, who had been a childhood friend of Diana's; Lord Romsey and his wife

Penny, whom they frequently holiday with; David Frost and his wife Carina, daughter of the Duke of Norfolk; Diana's sister Jane and her husband Robert Fellowes; and Diana's old flatmate Carolyn Bartholomew and her husband, William. He runs a party-catering company, and organized the private party that Charles had to celebrate his fortieth birthday. Most of these friends have young children, which helps bond them, and some are involved in both Charles's and Diana's charities, which adds a further dimension to their friendship. Penny Romsey, for example, had been an active member of Birthright even before Diana became patron; David Frost has done some dramatic fund-raising for Birthright, and has also hosted events like the Exhibition Tennis Tournament in aid of the Wishing Well Appeal; Gerald Grosvenor, the Duke of Westminster, is another. He was recruited by Charles in 1989 to run a target group on rural development for BitC.

Diana has conquered her fear of public speaking

The autumn of 1988 heralded a new era for the Prince, and it brought a change for the Princess too. In October, just ten days before *A Vision of Britain* was screened, Diana delivered her first proper speech for public consumption. Her previous speech, receiving the Freedom of the City of London the year before, had not had the public exposure of this one, and was of no great import. This one was. It was the Annual General Meeting of Barnardo's, held at the Queen Elizabeth II Conference Centre in Westminster, and delivered to a packed auditorium with press and television cameras present. Furthermore, she spoke on the subject about which everyone had longed to quiz her: the family and the needs of children.

Up to that point Barnardo's had simply provided services to children in need. It had never been a campaigning charity. It decided, however, the time had come to be more active, more outspoken, and to use its expertise to bring pressure to bear on government in the area of family legislation. The plan was to relaunch, to lose the 'Dr' label and shake off the orphan image, and Diana was asked, as their patron, whether she would help.

To Barnardo's surprise, she volunteered to make a speech. There were some things she wanted to say about family life, she said. Would that be appropriate? It was a

His 40th birthday was a turning point for Charles. A portrait taken at Highgrove

considerable coup; not only to provide a platform for the Princess to make her first speech, but to have her talk about the importance of a strong family unit when the world was busy speculating that her own was on the verge of disintegration. The new hard-hitting Barnardo's got off to the sort of start that no amount of money could ever have bought. The text of the speech went out two hours beforehand, so it would be in plenty of time for the morning papers, and a clip of Diana speaking was the number-one slot on both the 6 o'clock and 9 o'clock news on the BBC that evening.

She said:

Before accepting the presidency, I, perhaps like the majority of people, associated Barnardo's with orphans. This, as I have learnt during over fifty visits to projects throughout the United Kingdom, is inaccurate.

One aspect which has remained as a constant theme throughout is the enormous importance which Barnardo's attaches to family life. I fully realize that for many young people family life is not always a happy experience. They may have been thrown out of their homes or circumstances may have forced them to leave. Some are homeless; others are at risk of drug addiction or prostitution. It is even more of a challenge if such young adults are themselves parents.

I know that family life is extremely important, and as a mother of two small boys I think we may have to find a securer way of helping our children – to nurture and prepare them to face life as stable and confident adults. The pressures and demands on all of us are enormous. I do realize that the view of what constitutes a family is broader today than it was a century ago. Today few children lose parents through early death, but many do experience that loss through divorce and increasingly more complicated families result from separation and remarriage. These children's experience of family life may be different, but I do not believe it need necessarily be any less satisfying or effective.

Roger Singleton helped with the speech and, as is usual, provided a draft, but Diana wrote much of it herself, obviously bringing in ideas and lessons learned from her work with Relate; and also another charity in a similar vein, Turning Point.

Turning Point, set up in 1964, provides services for people with alcohol, drug and mental health problems, and has brought Diana face to face with some brutal facts of life since she became its patron in 1987. It is not a glamorous field. Much of the charity's work involves counselling young people whose lives have been wrecked by drug dependence, and families that have been brutalized and torn apart by alcohol abuse. She has even met psychopaths incarcerated in maximum-security psychiatric hospitals. Not many of their clients are interested in the etiquette of meeting a member of the Royal Family. There are not many curtsies to be seen in Rampton; nor even among Turning Point's staff. This is no slick charity, with a glamorous public-relations front and a prestigious mailing list.

Yet Diana is fascinated. She has become deeply involved in the work, loves talking to clients, and draws them out with the same skill she displays with Relate. She asks sensible, intelligent questions, the sort that counsellors might ask, and absorbs what she is told about methods and treatments. She also reads extensively round the subject of her own volition, watches television documentaries, and in the last four years has become very knowledgeable. Visiting a drug project one day, for instance, and talking to clients about where they got their supplies, and how the drug delivery system worked, she suddenly asked about crop substitution in Pakistan and Asia – a highly technical area that no one from Turning Point had briefed her on.

The result is that before a visit, staff and clients alike are often dismissive of her. Afterwards they always say how nice she was, how much she knew about the subject, and how well she related to people, in a way that was personable, understanding and sensitive. Some very staunch anti-monarchists have been completely won over by her. 'You're just not what I expected,' they have said time and again. So Les Rudd, chief executive, and a fairly unorthodox-looking character himself with an earring in one ear, never interferes, never stops people saying what they want. 'It's the risk she runs by meeting our clients,' he says, quite unashamed. 'She is here to try and understand their problems.'

Her interest has had a dramatic impact on a subject that has previously been a big turn-off to the public. Although it is a charity, Turning Point has always been dependent on statutory sources for 95 per cent of its funding. That money has come from central and local government grants. The public, so generous in appeals for starving children or endangered animals, have never been prepared to dig into their pockets for drunks and drug addicts: there has long been a stigma attached to this sort of problem, a popular perception that it is self-inflicted and sufferers, therefore, deserve everything they get. Until Diana became patron, Les Rudd firmly believed it was just not possible to raise money for their clients in the way that other charities did. Diana's involvement, however, has changed everything. The publicity her visits have aroused, and the speeches she has made on the subject, have helped to bring the issues out into the open and make people more aware that the dangers of drink and drugs are problems that concern all of us. It has also made them dig into their pockets. In the time that she has been patron, their fund-raising income has tripled.

Some £42,000 came in one night from the controversial première of the film *Buster*, about the Great Train Robbery, starring Julie Walters and Phil Collins. Charles and Diana had both been planning to attend, and the proceeds were to have been shared between the Prince's Trust, which organized the event, and Turning Point. A week before the showing, however, in October 1988, the Prince and Princess both pulled out, having apparently just realized the wisdom of not patronizing a film that glorified crime. By this time, however, the charities had sold the seats, their £42,000 apiece was safely theirs, and the publicity it all caused did them no harm at all.

It all went towards their £1 million Silver Jubilee Appeal, launched in January 1989. The aim throughout the year was to make industry recognize the problems of

drug and alcohol abuse within their own workforce, and take steps to help manage the problem. It was held at the Whitbread Brewery, a company that was already leading the field in helping its employees; and it was there again in May that Diana made another important and widely reported speech. Addressing a room full of employers, union representatives, government spokesmen and lawyers, she said:

> Those who imagine that drug and alcohol problems mainly affect the less fortunate members of our community would be quite wrong. On the contrary, addiction can strike any who suffer stress in their personal or professional lives. For alcohol and drugs do not respect age, sex, class or occupation and the line between recreational use and creeping addiction is perilously thin.
>
> We must remember, then, that the majority of Turning Point's clients come from ordinary communities. Very few of them resemble the stereotype junky or drunk. Most have – or certainly had – a normal family and working life. For many the tragic consequence of their addiction is that they have lost their jobs and hurt and confused their families.

Then, seizing the opportunity to air the subject of mental health, she said:

> I should also mention Turning Point's work in the field of mental health. As more mental patients leave hospital to join the community, there will be increasing demand on Turning Point's services.
>
> For people who have been in hospital for as long as they can remember, learning to fend for themselves can be a frightening experience.

Diana had just witnessed this for herself, during a visit to what is called a 'half-way house' in Nottingham. Alfred Minto House caters mostly for psychiatric patients who have been released from Rampton Special Hospital; in many cases residents have spent the best part of their lives in an institution. Having seen the house, and met and talked to the residents, she said she would like to see Rampton; would that be possible?

So Les Rudd organized a full half-day visit, and Diana became the first female member of the Royal Family to visit a Special Hospital, where some of the country's most dangerous psychiatric criminals are locked up. She visited three wards in the hospital and attended a seminar on the problems of discharging people from long-term mental institutions. There was a question and answer session afterwards, which prompted a lively debate about caring for people with mental-health problems in the community. She found the whole visit riveting, but it was a gruelling day. Rampton is a grim place, with long corridors and a series of locked doors. It can also be a dangerous place, and the atmosphere is very intimidating. Of the three wards Diana saw, one was mixed, men and women who were no danger to society and could have been successfully resettled in the community; another was a secure ward for men who had committed serious criminal offences; and a women's ward, which Diana found the most upsetting. The women were all severely mentally handicapped. The

Diana only takes on charities she feels she can really help.
Visiting a Help the Aged project in 1988

walls were padded and what furniture there was was padded too, so that the patients could safely work out their aggression on it. This group was highly unpredictable, and potentially a real security risk. A few of them came over and talked to Diana.

The hospital's medical director, Dr Diana Dickens, who showed her round, was filled with praise. 'My view is that she was brave,' she said. 'I've taken many visitors around the hospital and in that particular ward many are tense. Some of our patients are dangerous. They are very violent and very unpredictable people. She was so relaxed.'

What is more, she was scarcely out of the place before she made it known to Les Rudd that she would like to visit Broadmoor next.

Another visit, this time quite unpublicized, was to a residential project for 'chaotic' drug users in West London called ROMA. Turning Point's philosophy is that they neither criticize nor condone drug use. Abstinence is often the ultimate goal, but it is not the only goal; and at the ROMA project they care for people who have been on heroin, but are now taking methadone, an opiate substitute, on prescription. Most arrive with serious health problems, more often than not associated with HIV infection or full-blown AIDS, and a multitude of other problems. The object is to stabilize their health while they are there, counsel them on safer sex and safer drug use, advise them on diet and contraception, and help them to cope with illness and death.

Diana arrived at very short notice, and with no press. It was a private visit, to see the project for real, not with everyone on parade. A group discussion was going on when she arrived. The sixteen residents were sitting around, with one of them chairing the session, and a member of staff simply observing. Diana joined in. They were discussing one of their number, a punk with a strange hair-do and earrings, and how that person responded to the rest of the group's perception of him. Suddenly the chairman, who was a resident herself, turned the tables and focused everyone's attention on Diana. How did the group feel about royalty, she asked, and how did the Princess feel about their perception of her? It was completely unexpected, and the first time anything of the sort had ever happened to her.

Diana took the situation in her stride, and for the remaining thirty minutes of the session the focus was on her. She drew a comparison between her own position under the public spotlight, where she was regarded as being different from everyone else, and that of the punk they had just been discussing. She could identify with his feelings. Sometimes she found the pressure unbearable, sometimes she enjoyed it; just like the punk. He dressed that way because he enjoyed shocking people, and it gave him a kick; but there was a downside too; it was a terrible strain, she said, knowing that when she arrived anywhere and got out of the car, every camera was on her; what would happen if she fell over? Yet, at the same time, all that attention was exciting.

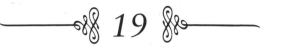

19

The Princess in the United States

The Princess of Wales is invariably happier talking to the lady who made the tea at any given event than the Lord Lieutenant of the county. She would rather visit a small town playgroup than take centre stage at a ceremonial banquet. She finds very formal occasions somewhat daunting, particularly if she is on her own. It is far easier to build up a rapport with ordinary people, like the tea lady or the ones she meets on walkabouts, because they are uninhibited in the way that children are, and ask the questions they want answers to – like, Where is your husband? How are the children? – which makes conversation simple. The dignitaries and people who meet her in more formal settings so often become tongue-tied, and do not know what to say. It is as if they feel they cannot talk about mundane matters, as they might when meeting any other stranger in similar circumstances, because she is a Princess and not part of the ordinary world.

At a gala dinner in New York in 1989, however, Diana discovered that the Americans have no such inhibitions. She was there as patron of the Welsh National Opera, who had been invited to perform at the Brooklyn Academy of Music. It was a prestigious invitation, the first time they had ever been to America, and it was very important for the company; but it was also going to be hugely expensive. The Brooklyn Academy has a good reputation for putting on interesting productions, and was the perfect venue, having been built specifically for opera; but it has only 2,200 seats, so the income they could expect to raise from selling tickets would inevitably be limited. The tour was going to cost almost a million pounds.

To the company's ineffable joy, the Princess said she would fly to New York to be there for the first night: without doubt, the most important night in its forty-three-year history. Furthermore, she agreed to a reception during the interval when people would pay to meet her, and to attend a dinner afterwards for a thousand people, who would each pay a thousand dollars for their meal and the privilege of eating it in the same room as the Princess of Wales. In one fell swoop the organizers could recoup the entire cost of the tour.

The dinner was held on the ground floor of the Wintergarden, and when Brian McMaster, director of the Welsh National Opera, toured the building in the morning, it seemed just like a giant shopping mall. It was hard to imagine it as anything else; but by evening the place had been transformed. It had been turned into the most sumptuous dining-room, fit for a Princess, laid up with tables for a thousand of New York's richest and most illustrious party-goers.

To Diana's dismay, the organizer had planned that she should make her entrance down a huge staircase – something she finds very unnerving, particularly when there are a thousand people below with their eyes firmly fixed on every step she takes. Brian McMaster was given the job of walking with her, and he was even more unnerved by the prospect and very tense, as Diana was aware. They had scarcely gone three steps, when the Princess muttered out of the side of her mouth, 'I'm going to fall down these steps.'

'No,' said Brian, 'it's me that does that sort of thing.'

Instantly the tension was gone, and they both sailed down the staircase without a hitch.

Diana loves meeting people on her walkabouts

The Wintergarden, New York 1989. 'I'm going to fall down these steps.'

The dinner was an experience neither of them will ever forget. As far as her fellow diners were concerned, Diana was the biggest film star they had ever come close to, and they were going to get their money's worth. Throughout the meal brash New Yorkers came up to talk to her, interrupted her as she was eating, wanting her to sign autographs, asking her personal questions, recounting their life story, saying she must meet their mothers-in-law. They were completely unstoppable. The Princess behaved with great poise and was polite and friendly to everyone, but her staff were on edge. Brian McMaster decided the only way to control the situation was to make his speech early, originally planned for after the dessert, so that Diana could escape quickly when the dinner was over.

'As I got up and moved across to the microphone,' recalls Brian, 'the woman who had organized the dinner nearly freaked. She had created a huge production number for the dessert. Hundreds of waiters were about to descend into the room down the staircase with the dessert sparkling in their hands.'

It had already been an eventful evening. Security at the Brooklyn Academy had been very tight. During the reconnaissance of the building, which Brian had done with Anne Beckwith-Smith and the security forces, they realized that during the interval the Princess would have to walk across the side of the stage to get from her box to the reception. Brian was a bit worried: *Falstaff* was a big production with three different sets, which took a very long time to change; the stagehands needed to work fast, and it might be tricky if the Princess was crossing the stage when they were trying to work.

'If anybody moves on stage while she's on it, he'll be shot,' said a security man. 'My men are good men, but . . .' Brian told the crew what he had been told with great relish; they all had a good laugh and thought nothing more about it.

During the performance, as he expected, there was an embarrassingly long pause between scenes, of five or ten minutes, when the lights came up in the auditorium. In the hope that she would not notice how long it was taking, Brian started talking to Diana, sitting beside him in the front of the box. Suddenly, the same security man from the reconnaissance earlier came up behind him and said, 'Get out of that chair.'

'I was in the middle of a conversation with the Princess, and I thought, I don't think this is exactly protocol. So I said, "I'm terribly sorry," and got up, and, without saying a word, the security man sat down where I had been sitting, and looked out at the audience.

'The Princess said, "This is stupid, nobody's going to shoot me here", but he didn't utter a word. I think he'd lost it, completely lost it. When the lights dimmed for the next scene he got up and left and still said not a word. No apology, nothing.'

There was strict security on the way out too. An IRA demonstration was in full swing outside the front of the Academy, so Diana was to leave by a side door and be driven away at full speed. Brian was to travel with the security men, in a car ahead of the Princess, and in order to speed their getaway he had to get into his car first, so that the second she touched the seat of her limousine the motorcade would shoot off.

'Look, I'm terribly sorry,' he said, explaining the problem to the Princess, 'but I've got to walk in front of you': something that of course is not normally done by anyone but the Prince of Wales. 'OK,' she said, 'don't worry.'

So he leapt into his car, and the Princess jumped into the car behind with Anne Beckwith-Smith, and there they sat, with the engines running for about ten minutes, while members of the New York police department screamed abuse at one another over walkie-talkies. It appeared the driver in the lead car was missing, and they were all so closely parked that nothing could move.

This was the first major foreign tour that the Princess had done on her own, without the Prince, and it was a triumph. She flew across on Concorde, and in the forty-eight hours she was in New York she carried out eight engagements, including visits to the AIDS paediatric wing of Harlem Hospital, a settlement for unmarried mothers and battered wives, a British toy trade promotion, and a Birthright reception. And as a result of the publicity and goodwill that was generated during that time, towards Wales in particular, at least one factory is now being built in the principality with American investment.

'Have you recovered from New York yet?' asked Brian McMaster when he next saw her.

'What do you mean?' said the Princess. 'It was great.'

Diana with America's First Lady, Barbara Bush, in Washington, 1990

In October 1990 Diana returned to America on a similar trip that was equally triumphant. It was another fund-raising dinner, this time in Washington, in aid of four charities, including the London City Ballet, the Washington Ballet and a home for children with AIDS. Diners were being asked to pay $2,500 for a ticket; a further $1,000 entitled them to attend a private reception beforehand at which the Princess was present. The event raised more than $320,000 for the four charities.

Members of the Royal Family are not supposed to do any active fund-raising, although these sort of events clearly go very close to the dividing line. The Americans are rather more up-front about it all than the British, and are not afraid to want value for money; but paying to meet the Prince and Princess has been happening in exactly the same way here for years. It's just that the British do not talk about it.

Shortly after Diana's visit to New York, she and Charles were at a Birthright ball at the Savoy to mark the hotel's centenary, with tickets sold at £1,000 a pair. It was a most exotic and extravagant affair, with wine specially flown in from Bordeaux, the famous Moulin Rouge dancers flown in from Paris for the cabaret, and the cream of London society in their ballgowns and finery. As usual, everything was meticulously planned in advance: the Prince would lead the way down the line-up of celebrities, with the Princess behind. Diana, however, destroyed the best-laid plans immediately and bounded ahead, leaving the Prince to follow.

'*Bonsoir, mademoiselle,*' Charles said to one of the can-can girls from the Moulin Rouge, shaking her warmly by the hand.

'I think I'd better stop you there, sir,' she said. 'I'm from Bexhill-on-Sea.'

There were all sorts of devices during the evening to raise money, including an auction. Vivienne Parry, Birthright's national organizer, was showing off a diamond brooch that had been donated, wafting it about in its box so that everyone could see what they were bidding for. Diana suddenly said, 'Vivienne, you've dropped it.' Sure enough, the brooch was on the floor, so she picked it up, put it back in its box, and sold it to a man for £17,500.

An hour later the man came looking for her with his brooch and said, 'There seems to be a diamond missing.' With

Carrying one of the Aids children for whom the Washington dinner raised money

Diana leads the way to the Moulin Rouge can-can girls at a Birthright ball at the Savoy, 1989

The Princess loves dancing, and takes to the floor with anyone who offers

mounting panic, Vivienne went back to the spot where she had dropped the brooch, which had had 250 people dancing on it in the meantime, and there was the diamond.

The Princess loves dancing and takes to the floor with anyone who offers on these occasions. The Prince is less keen, and does what duty demands. He will dance with his hostesses, and usually with the Princess, but it is not his favourite pastime. Diana has so much energy that she could happily dance the night away. At another Birthright event, the Red and Gold Ball at the Albert Hall back in 1986 – she wore a red dress, he wore a red watch strap – she nearly gave her detectives heart failure. There were 1,800 people there, and she disappeared on to the dance floor among them and vanished from sight. She danced with all sorts of people that night, so much so that it turned into a Princess of Wales Excuse Me Dance. The charity's accountant bet the Secretary of the Royal College of Obstetricians and Gynaecologists, which houses Birthright, £25 that he couldn't dance with the Princess, and he lost his bet. She scarcely left the floor.

Visiting an old people's home on one occasion, Diana was asked by a very elderly resident if she would dance with him. She did, and granted his dearest wish. It was typical. She frequently arrives for an engagement, which has been worked out in the finest detail beforehand, yet says, 'Is there anything you would like me to do?' She does not oblige everyone, however; she can be quite stubborn: lessons learnt from the Prince. Visiting the Brompton Hospital once, she was presented with a book written by one of the patients she visited. The press photographers all asked her to pose with the book, but she refused. But the people she is visiting are very different. She will put herself entirely at their disposal, especially the elderly. She has an instinctive feel for them and is immediately at ease in their company, because they too are uninhibited when they meet her. Charles has been patron of the Abbeyfield Society, a charity that provides homes for the elderly, for many years, and he too has an instinctive rapport with old people. It is an interest they share, and he too finds that the more ordinary and blunt they are with him, the better he responds.

Visiting an Abbeyfield house on one occasion he was told by an old lady, 'Young man, don't stand with your hands behind your back, it's bad for your posture.' Charles was delighted; he laughed and stood up straight as a rod.

Abbeyfield aims to prevent loneliness. It was started in 1956 by a Guards officer who was left some property in Bermondsey; when he went to look at it, he found an old man living there. Instead of kicking him out, he resigned from the Guards and invited a few more old men to live there too, and looked after the lot of them. He became known as the Scrubbing Major, and some thirty-five years later there are over 1,000 Abbeyfield houses in Britain where the same spirit applies. In each house seven or eight people, most of them over the age of eighty, live with a housekeeper, who provides meals and generally sees to their welfare. They have a room to themselves where they can put their own furniture and entertain at their liberty. They maintain their freedom and their dignity. The only qualification is that they must be reasonably ambulant. The whole idea is to provide old people with some companionship in their later years, and some loving care.

It is one of the Prince's favourite charities. Fifteen years ago he said that whenever he was in an area where there was an Abbeyfield house, he would try to visit it, and he has kept to his word. With over 1,000 houses in Britain it is almost a full-time job; and in the last four years they have become international too.

A new dimension that the Prince has brought to the charity is to introduce the concept to ethnic minority groups in Britain, where there is great need. Traditionally, ethnic families revere their elderly, and have taken care of them in their own homes, but they no longer have the space or the money to – the Western disease has taken hold. So in 1987 Charles held a lunch at Kensington Palace to which he invited Jean Cussons, chairman of the Council for Racial Equality; Trevor Hall from the Home Office; three members of Abbeyfield; two representatives from black organizations; and Harold Haywood, at that time still *in situ* at the Prince's Trust. Charles got straight to the point. There was a lot of ethnic deprivation in the inner cities. The Abbeyfield concept was neat, small and easy to handle, and he thought the ethnic minorities could do it for themselves. He wanted Abbeyfield to show them how: not do it for them, nor let the local authorities do it for them, but show them how to do it for themselves.

As a result of that lunch, the Abbeyfield concept now operates in a number of the ethnic communities. When their leaders discovered that the Prince of Wales was behind the idea, says Kaye Leverington, who helped set them up, 'They were ten feet tall, they were so proud.'

Comparing them both now with the time Kaye first met Charles and Diana together in 1981, she thinks they have learnt a lot from each other. Charles has taught Diana the ropes, and she has taught him to loosen up, to enjoy himself, and to relax. 'I wouldn't believe it if you told me they didn't have some godawful rows, they are both such strong personalities, but I'll tell you something: he is inordinately proud of her.'

Community Spirit

There is no doubt that after all his years of agonizing, the Prince of Wales does now play a very substantial role in life. He knows where he is going, knows that he serves a useful purpose, and is zealous to get on and do it. He has swept others along in the process; galvanizing people in areas that they had never thought concerned them. He even appears to have motivated government, particularly in dealing with the problems of youth unemployment. But there is also little doubt that the economic climate created by the Conservative government in the last decade has played a significant part in his success. Without the wealth that the enterprise culture and low taxation had produced in the private sector, there would have been no chance of persuading businessmen to finance social projects – still less of asking them to put environmental responsibility ahead of profit.

He may not have seen eye to eye with Margaret Thatcher, but the Prince had come a long way in his relationship with the ex-Prime Minister since Rod Hackney spilt the beans in October 1985 by saying that Charles feared he would inherit a country divided by 'haves and have-nots'. He had meetings with her quite frequently, and he and Diana were occasionally dinner guests at Number 10. They joined forces on a number of issues, in particular with the Prince's Youth Business Trust (PYBT), launched in November 1986. It was an amalgamation of two smaller similar ventures. Charles was keen to expand; at the same time, youth unemployment figures were soaring fast and becoming a national disgrace. Lord Young, then Secretary of State for Employment, was very worried, and wanted to put government money into a big job-creation scheme.

On the Prince's fortieth birthday, the PYBT launched a £40-million appeal which was to run for two years, in which the government promised to match pound for pound whatever sum the Trust raised. When it closed in March 1990, eight months ahead of schedule, they had reached their target. It is well on the way to becoming, as the Prince hoped, 'the biggest voluntary seed-corn finance operation anywhere in the world'. So far the Trust has helped set up over 8,000 new businesses.

Charles visits them regularly, and must be one of the greatest experts in the country on youth self-employment and the problems of job creation – not just in the inner cities, but in the rural communities too. He's intensely inquisitive; and never stops

Charles has not always seen eye to eye with Margaret Thatcher, but he and Diana were occasionally dinner guests at Number 10

agitating and worrying about whether things could be done better. He is the same with all his activities.

'Everyone's talking about the demographic change taking place,' he said one day. 'Is this going to make any difference? Don't you think there's a need to extend the age group? What if we went over twenty-six? What about people with disability, their education will have been retarded. Isn't there a case for the Trust extending its support to those people to the age of thirty?'

'When the Prince asks questions', says PYBT chief executive John Pervin, with the wisdom of one who has worked with Charles for some years, 'it is best to go away and think about it.'

Charles is still something of a thorn in the side of the government on environmental matters, but he no longer goes into open battle and at times he is very useful. He has had an ally, as well as a friend, in Chris Patten, former Secretary of State for the Environment. Chris Patten positively welcomed the Prince's attacks, because he used them as a bargaining lever with the Treasury.

The Prince is not party political. He does not believe that the problems of society are going to be solved by either a free market or a great state bureaucracy. He believes that the answer lies in partnership, in persuading the diverse parts of society to pull together. And the great thing he can bring to people in government is his time. He has time, which they do not have, to listen to what ordinary people are saying, and to study the issues.

In discussion with a group of businessmen one day, the Prince suggested tackling something man-sized. What about getting the private sector, he said, to lead the recovery of a whole town? He suggested Halifax could be the place, an old rundown textile town.

So a programme called the Calderdale Partnership was launched, and the first task was for the leaders of the business community and the local authority to work out ways of making their town prosperous again. Halifax very quickly went from a place of high unemployment to a place where there were actual skill shortages.

By 1988 Halifax could be seen to have recovered. The Prince finds the whole business incredibly exciting. It is here that all the strands of the last twenty years, all the diverse schemes that he has been talking about and working away at, are coming together. Regeneration involves architects and planners; it involves motivating young people; it involves small businesses and marketing; it involves looking after the needs of the elderly and disabled. It also involves looking after the environment. The message that he is pushing again and again to the business leaders is that their investment in society is not simply charity: it is sound business sense.

'Shareholders' interests', he says, 'are surely best served in the long term by creating a culture which is supportive of business, and by nurturing local communities which are more stable, safe and equipped with the best education and training possible.'

The Prince has not just been coercing others to invest in urban regeneration. The Duchy of Cornwall has recently bought a rundown site in Birmingham's famous jewellery quarter, which it is spending £2.5 million of its own money restoring. An even more exciting opportunity arose in the West Country. West Dorset Urban District Council wanted to expand the town of Dorchester, so it approached the Duchy of Cornwall, which owned Poundbury Farm, the 400-acre site they had in mind, to see whether it would make the land available for building. The Duchy agreed on condition that they built on the Prince's terms, thereby providing Charles with the perfect chance to put what he had been preaching into practice.

'I constantly read in the newspaper – when I do read a newspaper – that I am trying to create "a model village" or a "Dorset Utopia", but it is very far from the truth,' he has protested.

Nevertheless, Poundbury will incorporate many of the features that the Prince believes in. Local people have been consulted at every stage in the plans; it will be a traditional old-fashioned Dorset village with a traditional street pattern, and a mixed, self-sustained community; it will have low-cost housing alongside more expensive houses, with churches, shops, businesses and schools all nearby. The master-planner is Leon Krier, one of the architects involved in the alternative Paternoster Square scheme.

'It's not just a question of favouring old styles of architecture versus new ones,' Charles said, describing Poundbury to business leaders, '. . . but really a question of re-examining certain eternal principles and values which underlie and run through the whole human sense.' If applied in urban communities, they 'can result in more sympathetic and habitable places which have character and a degree of charm, and more than anything else, human scale, where people actually want to live, to work as well, and enjoy themselves'.

It is something of a stick and carrot approach that the Prince employs with government. His address to the World Conference on Saving the Ozone Layer, in March 1989, was typical; he began with his usual humour.

'I am delighted to have been invited . . . to speak. It makes an interesting change from talking to the multitude of different trees and plants in my garden and in my hothouse which, for those of you who don't have the pleasure of reading certain organs of the British press, is a serious occupation that is reputed to fill a substantial proportion of my time. As a result, Ladies and Gentlemen, I can assure you that there is absolutely nothing I don't know about the greenhouse effect.'

Then he went on to praise the government. 'The fact that the United Kingdom will meet the target of a 50 per cent reduction in CFC use ten years ahead of the 1999 deadline is something about which this country can be justifiably proud.

'CFCs do not just mean ozone depletion – they mean sea level rises, floods, heatwaves, droughts, changing monsoons and all the other consequences of greenhouse warming.'

It was actually the Prince who had made manufacturers move on the question of CFCs. The year before he had slipped into a speech at the Royal Society of Arts the fact that he had banned aerosols in his household. The newspapers ran the story that Charles had banished Diana's hairspray, and suddenly CFCs were in the public consciousness and demand for them dropped. He had achieved in one throwaway line what pressure groups had failed to do in years of campaigning.

Not all his remarks have been quite so well prepared. During an education conference in the summer of 1989 to deliver a pat on the back to teachers in the inner cities, Charles inadvertently insulted the very people he wanted to praise.

The Prince had sent a hundred chief executives to look at schools around the country and report on what they found. The real problem encountered was one of illiteracy.

'Illiteracy is not just a problem with the ethnic minorities,' said the Prince. 'It seems to be everywhere – even amongst my own staff. All the letters sent from my office I have to correct myself, and that is because English is taught so bloody badly.'

Quite unknown to him there were two journalists sitting in the audience. They could not believe their luck, and the following day the tabloids were predictably full of headlines like, 'Prince Slams Literacy', 'Own Staff Can't Spell', with angry reactions from the National Union of Teachers.

Charles was furious. He had thought he was speaking to an audience of educationalists, and had said what he said to illustrate a point in the context of how to raise attainment in schools. He had not meant to insult anyone, and was deeply embarrassed, particularly concerning his own staff. There were some very strict rules drawn up after that about where and when journalists might go.

Diana and Charles in Spain on an official tour in April 1987. Plenty of foreign trips, but no more cocktail parties

It was not the first time he had been put on the spot by journalists. It was always the custom on foreign tours for the Prince and Princess to hold a cocktail party, usually on the first evening of their stay in another country, to which they invited accredited members of the press who had travelled with them, and a number of press from the host country too. Most of the British press corps are regulars; some, like Jayne Fincher, who took the photographs for this book, have been following them faithfully for the last ten years, and both Charles and Diana are quite friendly towards them. Jayne was invited to take exclusive photographs for the Prince's fortieth birthday, which she took at Highgrove. While she was there the Princess noticed that, like her, Jayne bit her nails, and they compared notes on how awful their hands looked and how difficult it was to stop. (Interestingly, Diana has now stopped.)

The cocktail parties were very informal occasions, but on the strict understanding that everything said was 'off the record', said in confidence and not to be reported. On their tour of Spain in April 1987, the party was held at the El Prado Palace outside Madrid; the Prince found himself in a conversation with a Spanish reporter, in which he spoke quite frankly about living with the constant fear of the IRA. The reporter went straight back to his newspaper, and the Prince's thoughts on the IRA were plastered all over the Spanish press the following day. Once it had appeared there, the British press felt free to follow suit. Since then, there have been dozens of foreign tours, but absolutely no more cocktail parties.

The Growing Children

Aware that Diana did not much enjoy public speaking, the British Deaf Association wrote a short speech for her to launch the BDA's centenary year. The Princess sent it back saying it was too short, so they wrote a longer one. When she rose to her feet at the Mansion House in February 1990 to address 200 top executives, they scarcely recognized a word of it.

Speaking of the untapped potential that 7 million people in Britain with hearing loss represented, she said:

> Because deafness is invisible, it is all too easy for this potential to be overlooked by the hearing world. And, with so many good causes competing for attention, it is hard to be sympathetic to a handicap which you can't even see, hard to imagine the frustration felt by deaf people whose intellectual and physical talents are so often obscured by communication problems, and harder still to imagine the loneliness of deaf children, 90 per cent of whom have parents who can hear.
>
> The BDA has done much to promote the special culture represented by all forms of deaf communication, especially British Sign Language. But whichever medium is used, the message is the same: the deaf community wants to play a full part in society. Deaf people are not asking for sympathy, only for a fair chance to live and contribute as full members of society.

Speaking through an interpreter, Chairman John Young and his wife Lilian Lawson, also deaf, said they had been astonished by the Princess's speech – 'She had done her own research'. The effect was miraculous. Not only did several people approach the BDA and offer their services, but an Under Secretary to the Minister of Education said he wanted to arrange a meeting because he was very interested in what the Princess had said about the education of children, and he wanted to look into it. For years the BDA had been running a campaign to improve the education of deaf children and had got nowhere. The Princess of Wales stood up and mentioned the subject in a five-minute speech, and suddenly the Minister was interested.

Diana has made a huge difference to the deaf community. Before her involvement, the BDA had never tried special events to raise money. In the last five years Diana has brought them into the public eye with a series of glamorous gala first nights, and

donations have risen dramatically. First there was the James Bond film, *A View to a Kill*, in 1985, which she and the Prince attended together; the proceeds from this were shared with the Prince's Trust, but it raised £45,000 for the BDA. There were no sub-titles for the deaf, but they had been given a synopsis of the plot to read beforehand.

At the royal première of the Bolshoi Ballet's *Ivan the Terrible*, at Covent Garden the following year, Diana was acutely aware of the problem. Meeting Sallie Holmes, the deaf wife of the vice-chairman of the BDA, she asked how she would be able to follow the ballet: 'She asked if it was the vibrations that helped. I was able to reassure her that the rhythm of movements in ballet is music in my eyes; also, there is history in a play like *Ivan the Terrible*.' The film version of *Children of a Lesser God*, a story about a man falling in love with a deaf girl, was ironically no easier. It was an American film, given its première in 1987; it used American sign language, which those

Diana attending the Moscow State Circus in 1988. The child ended up sitting on Diana's lap to watch the circus

deaf in Britain were unable to understand. Once again, the Prince and Princess were together that evening, and the proceeds were shared between the British Deaf Association and the Variety Club.

Diana's responses are instinctive. Before the start of the Moscow State Circus, in 1988, a little deaf girl presented her with a bouquet of flowers. 'Where's the little girl who gave me the flowers?' she said, as she sat down in the royal box, which had a splendid view of the ring. Ten-year-old Shazir Nasreen was brought over, and ended up sitting on the Princess's lap throughout the circus. On another occasion in the same year, she was presenting awards for Young Deaf Achievers at the Grocers' Hall. As soon as she sat down, she spotted five-year-old Lucy Smith, who was partially blind as well as deaf, starting to get up from her table to bring over a bouquet. Diana immediately sprang to her feet, and walked over to the little girl's table to take the flowers and save her the journey.

In 1989 Barnardo's launched its first major campaign, to increase public aware-ness about the needs of young mentally handicapped people as they grow into adulthood. The provisions for them are pitiful, and their chances of finding employ-

Holidaying in Majorca as the guests of the Spanish royal family has become a regular event

ment, given the present attitude on the part of employers, government and the public, are poor. The campaign was in the form of a charter called 'If you let me', and Diana was asked whether she would be the first to sign it. She would not only sign it, she said, but suggested doing so at Kensington Palace, with a small selection of the press present; thus she invited three young people, who suffered from mental handicaps and embodied the need they were trying to draw attention to, to come and present it to her.

One was Gerald, a garrulous sixteen-year-old living in residential care in Northern Ireland, which usually ends there at the age of eighteen. He was about to leave school and his job prospects were grim. With his handicap he would not fit into any youth-training scheme, and his school and social services could think of nothing else. Another was Donna, a young woman of twenty-two who had been cared for by Barnardo's for most of her life; she had been written off at one time, but now has a job in a hotel in Harrogate. The third was a profoundly handicapped nineteen-year-old from Liverpool called Mandy, for whom quality of life was her greatest need.

Gerald was a little fazed when he met the Princess. He had chatted away happily on breakfast television earlier that morning, but by the time he was introduced to the Princess of Wales he had rather lost his tongue.

'Tell the Princess what happened to you yesterday, Gerald,' said Roger Singleton. 'You did a couple of things you've never done before, like going on an aeroplane.'

It did the trick. Gerald found his tongue and his confidence, and in no time at all was bored with the charter signing ceremony. He began to wander around and

The Trooping of the Colour has been one of the young Princes' rare formal public appearances

The most exciting part of the day – watching the RAF fly-past from the balcony of Buckingham Palace

started to follow the dogs, Tigger and Roo, into the room next door, which was Diana's private study. The first time he was retrieved, but he was determined. Realizing what was going on, Diana said, 'Don't worry, leave him.' Then she followed him in herself and they were both gone for five minutes or more, while he had a good look at everything, and Diana showed him pictures of William and Harry, who were both at school that morning.

After forty-five minutes or so, Roger Singleton decided they ought to make a move, but Gerald beat him to it. 'I've got to go now,' Gerald said, coming up behind the Princess and holding her by the arms.

'Right,' said Diana, 'that's fine. Thank you for coming.' And she went downstairs with them all, and waited in the courtyard outside until all the wheelchairs were loaded into the mini-van and everyone was aboard, before waving goodbye.

Gerald's haste had been to make sure he got to travel in the front seat.

Up until last year, William and Harry were kept firmly out of the public eye. Their only formal public appearances were at the annual Trooping of the Colour ceremony in June, when they travel in a state landau and join the rest of the Royal Family on the balcony at Buckingham Palace for the most exciting part of the day, the RAF fly-past. Occasional visitors to Kensington Palace or Highgrove would encounter them, but it was usually a chance meeting. Recently, however, the Princes have gradually started appearing with their parents at early-evening receptions. Guests arriving are astonished to find two little hands stretching up to be shaken at

Prince William playing with his mother's handbag during a polo match in 1989

the end of the line-up and, if anyone misses them out, the hands pursue them until they have been shaken.

'I hope you don't mind that I've brought my children,' is often how the Princess introduces them. They stay for a while, have a glass of orange juice, and disappear quietly when it is time for bed. Sometimes visitors are treated to the entire family, although more often they are with their mother. However, there have been occasions when Diana has been away for a weekend with her mother, and Charles has been left in charge. On these occasions, the boys have helped him entertain guests at Highgrove.

The fact that the Prince spends so much time away does nothing to diminish the affection the boys have for their father; in fact, quite the reverse. They get terribly excited at the prospect of seeing him, especially when they hear his helicopter coming. They go racing across the park at Highgrove to leap into his arms, as often as not covering his smart city suit with sheep dung that they have trodden in in their haste. 'The number of times I've had to go and get changed the minute I arrive home,' he says.

Now that the boys are a little bit older, Charles and Diana feel they should gently start involving them, to prepare them for the life that is ahead. When the Princess launched the National Hospital's £9.5 million rebuilding appeal at the Guildhall in 1987, John Young sent her a copy of the video that had been made of the occasion. He had a letter back from the Princess saying, 'I made William sit down and look at it with me – I thought it was time he should see this sort of thing – and we were both fascinated.'

But it is a gentle introduction, and they are still keeping what the Princes do down to a minimum. They had been adamant about not involving them in the Wishing Well Appeal and, when the Prince was asked to make a second television documentary with Christopher Martin, this time on the environment, he thought long and hard about bringing the boys into it, but in the end decided against it.

There is no hope of keeping the young Princes hidden from the press, however. Both boys have become quite blasé about photographers and, although they are *usually* as scrupulously polite as their parents, Harry has been known to stick out a mischievous tongue. The press have been given firm rules about when and where they can take photos, such as at the beginning of school terms or sports day. They often get less formal shots of them watching polo in the summer, travelling to and from Balmoral, and with the Queen and other members of the Royal Family at church at Sandringham on Christmas morning.

Ten years on, Royal Family gatherings are less of a strain for Diana. She and the Queen have far more in common today than they did when Diana was first married – not least of all, the children. The Queen is a doting grandmother. She is also impressed by how well brought up the boys are; and she has nothing but admiration for the way the Princess has taken on such a gruelling work-load. The Duke of Edinburgh has always been enchanted by Diana, and she gets on remarkably well with the rest of the family too – especially Prince Andrew

The Queen is a doting grandmother. Taking Prince Harry back to Windsor Castle for lunch after church on Easter Sunday

and Prince Edward, who are of much the same age. And they have friends in common: William Bartholomew, Carolyn Pride's husband, is a friend of Edward's, so they do all see each other on a fairly regular basis. The extended family is close too. The Gloucesters are neighbours at Kensington Palace, and also Princess Margaret, whom Diana gets on well with, as she does with her children, especially Lady Sarah Armstrong-Jones. Princess Margaret shares Diana's love of ballet and, as another who has bucked the system in her time, she has always been supportive of her. The nearest Diana has come to a clash with any member of the family is with Princess Anne, an extremely hard-working, outdoor, no-nonsense sort of woman, who had a simple clash of personality with the superstar that had arisen in their midst; but even this relationship has improved as they have both grown older.

Diana has mellowed; she is secure and confident now, and has proved to be as hard-working and effective as her sister-in-law. She is no longer fighting the system, and no longer allows herself to get trapped at Balmoral. Their regular family holiday in Majorca with the Spanish royal family has solved this problem. The Princess not only loves the sunshine, but finds King Juan Carlos and his family good fun to be with.

Quite often when the Prince and Princess are in Scotland they stay with the Queen

'One of those rare people whose touch can turn everything to gold.' For Charles, his grandmother has always been special

Mother at Birkhall, and not at Balmoral. The Queen Mother has always been a great fan of Diana's and the feeling is entirely reciprocated. For Charles, of course, his grandmother has always been special. In a foreword to a book about her, he once wrote, 'Ever since I can remember, my grandmother has been the most wonderful example of fun, laughter, warmth, infinite security and, above all, exquisite taste. For me, she has always been one of those extraordinarily rare people whose touch can turn everything to gold.'

The Queen Mother has never been one to let sentiment get in the way of business, though, even in her ninetieth year. Last spring, when Charles bought some Aberdeen Angus calves from her, which she breeds at the Castle of Mey, to start up an organic herd at Highgrove, there was some hard bargaining to be heard over the price.

Setting-up costs were so high, in fact, that the Prince has had to have half pedigree cows in the herd, and half cross-bred. Originally, he wanted to have rare breeds wandering about in the parkland to gaze out on, but he and his farm manager, David Wilson, went to look at some at the Cotswolds Rare Breed Centre and were rather put off.

'They had hugely long horns, great wide handlebar affairs,' says David, 'and they eyed us in a very peculiar way. We decided they were not for the parkland. Aberdeen Angus are naturally polled, and they're pretty placid, so we have gone for them.'

The Prince has always had romantic ideas about his livestock. His dairy herd are Ayrshires because he thinks they are so much prettier than the ubiquitous black and white Friesians. He would have had Jerseys, but the milking machinery already in place at the farm when he bought it would not have fitted them, and it was too expensive to replace. During a painting holiday in the hills of Tuscany in 1986 he was seized with another idea: cowbells, so he could listen to the gentle tinkle from his bedroom window. So a shipment of antique brass cowbells on wooden collars was sent over from Italy, which sent the cows into a complete frenzy, and his neighbours reaching for ear-plugs.

His organic beef herd arose out of a visit in July 1989, suggested by Alan Gear, to Richard Young's organic beef farm in Broadway. The Youngs' farm, where Richard's mother, Mary, rules the roost, is idyllic: the herd roams freely and naturally over the hills with minimum interference, and when a mother calves, the calf suckles and runs with the herd – so several generations are living together. They have very low veterinary bills and the cows are content. At the end of the process, the slaughtering is as important, in the Young philosophy, as their lifestyle. One of the family travels with the animals to a small local slaughterhouse and remains with them to the end, so they suffer as little stress as possible. The process of being loaded on to a lorry and driven even a few miles is very stressful in itself, so Richard's sister, Rosamund, has plans to set up a mobile abattoir, which would drive from farm to farm so that animals would not have to go through the trauma of being transported at all. Charles is very interested in Rosamund's idea, but he is concerned that new EC legislation will mean that in the future there will just be a few giant slaughterhouses, which will take in animals from hundreds of miles around.

There are also plans for the dairy herd to become organic in time. The whole process of transferring to organic methods has been gradual, partly because of the need for the farm to pay its way, and partly because of the strict rules laid down by the Soil Association. But the organic movement has taken off so comprehensively in the last couple of years that farmers are getting more for organic produce than their conventional crops, and it is becoming economically very attractive. In 1990 organic wheat was fetching £250 a ton compared with £180 a ton for conventional wheat; and with no chemical sprays and fertilizers, it was costing the farmer half the amount the conventional farm needed to spend to produce it.

The Prince sold his entire first crop to Tesco's for bread which it marketed as the 'Highgrove Loaf', selling at 59 pence for 400 grams, although in fact less than half the wheat in it came from Highgrove. Three pence from every loaf sold went to charity, but the decision to sell to a supermarket giant rather than supporting local bakeries was a opportunity curiously missed.

22

One World

Alan Gear was sitting at his desk one morning early last year when the telephone rang.

'Mr Gear,' said a voice, 'please save me from the Prince of Wales.'

It was Kevin Knott, deputy secretary of the Duchy of Cornwall, whose day had just been shattered by the news that the Prince of Wales intended to turn the Duchy into a peat-free area.

'We have a world-famous nursery that produces pot plants sold all over the country. What on earth are they going to do if they can't use peat?'

Kevin's life could never be called dull. The Prince constantly has new ideas, and wants them implemented or investigated immediately. There is no respite even when he is abroad; he telephones from the other side of the world with a new thought or instruction, or to see what progress has been made with the last one. The reception he gets from the deputy secretary is not always enthusiastic. Kevin is classically trained in land management and, like his late father-in-law Sir John Higgs, has had a healthy scepticism for some of the Prince's less orthodox ideas. On this occasion, it was the nurseryman's staple that the Boss was gunning for: peat.

The Royal Society for Nature Conservation, of which Charles was patron, had persuaded him to launch a campaign to save Britain's lowland peat bog, a richly varied and scarce wildlife habitat, which was being drained, dug up and scattered about in people's gardens at such a rate that 98 per cent of it had already disappeared.

Charles was keen to help, but instead of just casting doom, he wanted to be able to offer an alternative to Britain's gardeners; thus he turned to the Henry Doubleday Research Association for help. They had been arguing against the use of peat in horticulture for some years and had also been experimenting with alternatives. So when the anti-peat campaign was launched in April 1990, it was a joint venture, and 100,000 copies of a leaflet about suggested alternatives had vanished within three months. In the meantime, one of their staff had been down to the Duchy nursery to advise on what to use instead.

Charles had become interested in the vegetable gene bank at Wellesborne, funded largely by Oxfam, and had had several seed varieties from it, which he had grown at Highgrove, including purple carrots. The latest were purple Brussels sprouts.

Charles and Diana on a visit to Hungary in March 1990

Charles felt strongly that it was not just fruit that was in danger; government should be responsible for ensuring the future of all gene banks. The arguments were irrefutable. Addressing an International Conference of the Rare Breeds Survival Trust in 1989, he had said as much, and secured the future of Wellesborne:

'In 1960 a child suffering from leukaemia had only a one in five chance of remission. Now, thanks to two potent drugs prepared from a tropical forest plant called the rosy periwinkle, the child enjoys nine chances in ten. How many other plants are there with this sort of potential – perhaps facing extinction in the rain-forest – where there is the greatest concentration of species under threat?'

The Prince was warming up for a lecture of major importance on the rain-forest, delivered in the Royal Botanic Gardens at Kew in February 1990:

Once a rain-forest or a species living in it is gone, it is gone for ever. The phrase 'Now or never' has never been used with more chilling accuracy than when applied to the task of saving the remaining rain-forests.

Their role in controlling aspects of our climate is so great that they can truthfully be said to affect every single person alive today, let alone future generations.

For hundreds of years the industrialized nations of the world had plundered the forests for their natural wealth, he said, and also the people who depended upon them:

Ever since the first explorers from Spain and Portugal set foot in South America, and the British visited the Caribbean, the people of the so-called 'developed world' have always treated tribal people as total savages, be it to enslave them, subdue, 'civilize' them, or convert them to our way of religious thinking. Even now, as the Penan in Sarawak are harassed and even imprisoned for defending their own tribal lands, and the Yanomami in Brazil are driven into extinction by measles, venereal disease or mercury poisoning following the illegal invasion of their lands by gold prospectors – even now, that dreadful pattern of collective genocide continues.

It was a long and learned lecture, delicately written around a highly political and contentious subject, although at times not written delicately enough. The Malaysian government is still smarting from the Prince's reference to genocide in Sarawak. They regarded it as a serious breach of diplomatic etiquette. But it was a lecture spoken straight from the heart. The Prince was fresh from the Indonesian rain-forest, and much of it was from first-hand knowledge.

He had been to Indonesia with Diana in November 1989, on their first trip to Asia, which included a potentially hostile visit to Hong Kong. It was thought the residents might use the royal visit to register their protest over 1997, when Britain's lease of the colony expires and the capitalist mecca reverts to communist China. As it was, they did no such thing – Charles and Diana were fêted as jubilantly in Hong Kong as they have been everywhere else. Charles had been there ten years before, but Diana had never been there, and was stunned by the number of people. Nearly 6 million people

The Sultan's Palace, Indonesia. Formal occasions can be daunting

live in Hong Kong, about 21,000 people to every square kilometre, the highest density in the world and the most crowded place in history.

Indonesia was even more of a culture shock. It is a country of extremes. The Sultan's Palace in Central Java was comparatively opulent, albeit insufferably hot and humid – so much so that during a dancing display in their honour, Diana was blowing at her fringe to try and cool herself and get a little air circulating. The dancers were exquisitely dressed in brilliant colour, and the Palace adorned with elaborate carvings. But elsewhere there were some of the worst scenes of poverty and overcrowding that either of them had ever witnessed. In an area of Jakarta known as Grogol, a shanty-town where Charles officially switched on a new water pump installed by a British company, hundreds of thousands of people were living beside stinking canals in which they washed and swam, and drew water for drinking and cooking. An important part of any foreign visit is promoting British business. In Indonesia, the Prince gave a reception and lunch for British defence salesmen, which the Indonesian Minister for Defence attended. Some of the salesmen had been waiting six months to see the Minister; Charles paved the way. Diana's role abroad is essentially goodwill and public relations. She charms and enchants her hosts at the banquets and receptions, and flatters them by her interest in their social problems.

An afternoon spent visiting the sick and poor, including a leprosy hospital on this occasion, goes a long way in sealing relations. Fascinating as the trip was, it had some harrowing moments.

In both Hong Kong and Indonesia Charles snatched a few hours here and there to do some filming for his environmental film. For ten months in all, producer Christopher Martin and a BBC film crew followed him round the world, pursuing the 'art of the possible', seizing precious hours in the Prince's schedule to film in the Flow Country, the Highlands of Scotland, Rome, Washington DC, Florida, and in parts of England. The film was to be part of One World Week in May 1990, when the BBC joined up with international networks to bombard their viewers with worries about the environment. It was a natural subject for the Prince, but he was hesitant at first. There were people who knew far more on the subject than he did, he argued; he was not a scientist, not really qualified for the job. In the end he decided to go ahead with the film, but to take the philosophical route: not to look at the issues, but to look behind the issues; to question man's position on earth, and try and make people realize that it is not governments who are going to save the planet, but individuals.

By the time it was shown, on the Wednesday evening of One World Week, the viewing public had had a surfeit of environmental problems, and many people were also baffled. *A Vision of Britain* had been about buildings that everyone could identify with: people in their living-rooms understood what the Prince was saying, and felt they had a spokesman. *The Earth in Balance* was an entirely different matter. It was too philosophical to be as popular as the previous one had been, but it was a powerful film with a heartfelt message, reinforced with teachings from history, mythology and the various religions of the world. It was the Prince of Wales laid bare – a cry for help, a solemn plea for mankind to think again and change its values before we all perish:

> We really can move mountains and erase whole forests in the twinkling of an eye – but science and technology still can't put them back as they were. This has happened just at a time when we seem to have lost the ancient sense of kinship with nature which – not so long ago – was instinctive to us. That resulting imbalance has led, I believe, to a crisis of the spirit – or, perhaps, a 'loss of soul'.
>
> Do we not, most of us, feel a profound, almost unconscious unease at the course we have all been taking, almost as if we were living on borrowed time; desperately rushing, exploiting, doing, expecting others to come after us to clear up the mess; as if after a wild adolescent party which has gone terribly wrong.
>
> . . . the consequences to our children if we should fail are almost unimaginable.

One of the television critics, intending to be rude, called the film 'ethereal'. Far from being offended, the Prince was pleased with the word. He was quite unapologetic about the stance he had taken. There had been long discussions beforehand about whether the British public would be able to stomach so lofty a film, but he had said, 'I am not an expert, but I do have strong feelings and not to expose them would be an act of cowardice.'

Unlike the film about architecture, people in their living-rooms had no concept of what it was like to be in places like Grogol and see the squalor for themselves. He could talk about the awesome population problem – 'By the end of the year there will be over 90 million more of us than there were when it began' – and the terrifying poverty of the underdeveloped world, which was paying out more in interest repayments on its debt than it was receiving in aid.

Charles did see it all at first-hand; and is frustrated by everything he sees. In March he and Diana were in West Africa, on a trip to Nigeria and the Cameroon where once again they were treated to two very different styles of life – the presidential grandeur and the appalling poverty – and again they visited a leper hospital. The Prince is only too aware that many of the problems about the rain-forests and the developing world are

Diana visiting a deaf school in Cameroon. It is a country of extremes

not environmental at all, but political, and there is only so much he can say, as he discovered when he spoke about Sarawak.

It was important on the environmental issue, he realized, to alter fundamental attitudes, and where better to start than in the business community. In February, at very short notice, he convened a meeting in Charleston in Carolina, for 120 chairmen and chief executives from all over the world. Declaring himself merely a 'catalyst', he posed question after question, issue after issue, for which he wanted written answers. People there commented that no one else in the world, not even the President of the United States, could have got so many top people together at such short notice.

The Prince said: 'How are we going to tackle the huge challenges facing us – vast population growth rates, poverty, hunger, mass migrations, environmental degradation, potential conflict over diminishing natural resources – unless business, with its presence in these crucial areas and with so many people, their children and families, revolving around such business, takes a long-term view.'

He had chosen Charleston for the venue, partly because he loves the American example; he feels it is the source of extraordinary energy, a big, generous country where people dream the undreamable, and don't agonize too much about why things don't work, but instead move on to the next idea. And partly because of the community spirit he felt the town embodied.

The next date in his diary for May 1990 was a visit to Hungary with the Princess, another country in the Eastern bloc where communism had been toppled. He suggested the business leaders come too. Here was a prime example of how the business community could bring about international solutions. They had the expertise in helping to develop small businesses, the ability to show the Hungarians the way. It was a formula that he felt could be applied anywhere.

'Central Europe,' said the Prince, 'has itself been the victim of ideological experiment and the worst follies of a command economy. Its very landscape bears the dreadful scars and so do its children. We are only just becoming aware of the terrible catastrophe you have been suffering. Somehow we must find a way to help reverse this apparent ecological Armageddon.'

In the meantime, Diana had a busy schedule of her own, the most moving and interesting event of which was a visit to the Peto Institute, where doctors have developed a revolutionary method for treating children who suffer from cerebral palsy. Children go there from all over the world for the treatment, several from Britain, and as Diana met some of them and chatted to their parents, she struggled to fight back the tears on several occasions. The Institute, founded by Professor Andreas Peto, who died in 1967, is now run by Dr Maria Hari, a tiny figure reminiscent of Mother Teresa. Before she left, the Princess pinned an honorary OBE on Dr Hari's lapel. Once again, Diana presented the human face to their tour that complemented the Prince's tougher, more intellectual stance. It was a visit that they both enjoyed enormously, and where they took obvious pleasure from each other's company.

Their relationship was as good as it had ever been. Success brought contentment, and the worries that had tortured Charles were in decline. He had found Charleston exciting. He could see the way forward, could see how it all might be made to work, how the ills of the world could be put to rights, how important it was to think in the long term, and think globally. The disparate strands of his life were in fact all part of a much larger whole, and the answers were within his grasp.

Armed with his new-found vision, he went to Trieste in March and dropped a bombshell to the United World Colleges (UWC) International Council. As 172 delegates from twenty-five countries settled back to hear how their great organization should greet the 1990s, their president bluntly told them the time had come for change. They were no longer relevant to the needs of the modern world. What had been appropriate in the post-war period, when peace and international understanding were paramount, was now elitist and outmoded, and it was impossible to raise finance for it. Instead of influencing a few people very deeply and 'producing a succession of lawyers, economists and businessmen', they needed to be looking to the problems of the Third World, and teaching people how to combat hunger and drought, while appreciating 'the delicate balance of nature'. They should be 'harnessing the knowledge of so-called primitive societies before such ancient wisdom is lost to mankind for ever'. He told his audience, who had devoted much of their lives to promoting the UWC ideal, that if they did not like the idea they could say goodbye to their president.

His example was the Simon Bolivar Agricultural United World College in Venezuela, which had come into being following an official visit to Venezuela in 1978. He had met a group of ex-UWC students while he was there, who said that what was needed was an agricultural college to tackle the problem of the drift from the land to the cities, which had left a chronic shortage of farmers – not just in Venezuela, but all over South America. Ten years later the college was fully operational. Charles had been to see it for the first time in February 1989 and sent Stephen O'Brien and Julia Cleverdon from BitC to go and have a look too.

'Tell me what I can do to support it,' he said. 'Does it make sense?'

Filled with doubt, he asked Julia to join him in Trieste. 'Please come and listen to what I'm going to say to them because I don't think they're going to like it.'

He was right, they did not. Headmasters and ex-students alike were deeply offended. 'The secondary vision sounds very worthwhile,' said one elderly gentleman rising to his feet to argue, 'but the primary vision must be kept going.'

'It's all very well saying that,' said Prince Charles with a flash of anger, 'but I'm the one who's got to raise the money, and I'm telling you it can't be raised.'

23

The Broken Arm

One fateful Thursday afternoon last June, the calm and tranquillity in the royal couple's life was shattered. In the midst of a polo match at Cirencester Park, his pony stumbled. Charles lost his balance and crashed heavily to the ground, badly breaking his right arm in two places above the elbow. It was to blight the rest of his year, and revive all the old rumours about both his state of mind and the state of their marriage.

Diana was in London at the time. She was told immediately that there had been an accident, but was told there was no point in rushing to his side. It was not life-threatening. Charles was in pain, but had been taken to the casualty department of the local hospital, where he had insisted upon waiting his turn to be seen by a doctor. He had also spoken to Diana on the telephone and convinced her that there was nothing to panic about. No one realized at that stage how severe the fracture was.

So Diana stayed in London and carried on with her plans. There were two dates she particularly wanted to keep. Anne Beckwith-Smith was having a leaving party in the early evening, to which all the directors and organizers of the Princess's charities that she had come to know over the years had been invited. Diana wanted to be there, as a token of her thanks for ten years' friendship and hard work, knowing it would mean a lot to Anne. She spent more than an hour at the party, telling anyone who asked about the Prince's broken arm, the news of which had been on the late afternoon news, 'It's a rough game; it was bound to happen some time'. Afterwards, she had arranged to accompany Carolyn Bartholomew to see Puccini's *La Boheme* at Covent Garden; she had bought the tickets and did not want to let her friend down.

Before the end of the performance, however, news had reached her that there were serious complications, and the fracture was far worse than they had at first realized. Visibly upset, Diana apologized to her friend for abandoning her, then slipped away and raced down to Cirencester Hospital where Charles was just coming round after a forty-five-minute procedure in which the local orthopaedic surgeon, Mr Bruce Morris, manipulated the broken bone under anaesthetic and set his upper arm in plaster. Before doing any kind of operation, Mr Morris wanted to see if this would work.

The Prince came out of hospital three days later, on Diana's twenty-ninth birth-

Leaving hospital in Cirencester after the Prince's polo accident on Diana's 29th birthday

'It's a rough game, it was bound to happen some time.'

day, with his arm in a sling, but feeling reasonably cheerful. He was not sleeping well because it was painful and difficult to move, but otherwise he felt fine, and saw no good reason why he should not carry on regardless. After his first outing, however, in a helicopter, to the Parachute Regiment for their annual celebration, he thought again. He was quite shaken by the day's events, and decided it would be sensible to cancel his immediate engagements; to stay at Highgrove and have people come to him. Where groups were disappointed, such as young PYBT entrepreneurs whose exhibition he had had to miss, he invited them down to Highgrove so he could talk to them there. Most speeches had to go by the board.

In the meantime, Diana stepped up her own work-load, standing in for Charles whenever possible, as more and more engagements were cancelled. One date he did not miss, and would not have missed if it had meant arriving in a Bath chair, was his grandmother's ninetieth birthday on 4 August. He had organized a concert in her honour at Buckingham Palace, for which he had specially commissioned three pieces, one for the cello which was played by Rostropovitch, as well as putting together a collection of all her favourite pieces. He began the proceedings by saying that he had puzzled over how to make something special for his wonderful grandmother, and here was what he had come up with. It was a charming evening, a warm and touching tribute to the Queen Mother, surrounded by all the people whom she loved most, her children and grandchildren, as well as some very old and dear friends, courtiers and a few favoured outsiders.

A few days later the Prince went off to Majorca for a holiday in the sun with King Juan Carlos again. It got off to a disastrous start. Arriving on the island a few days ahead of Diana and the boys, who had an appointment at the circus, he found himself in a high-speed car chase. Spanish photographers pursued his car at speeds of up to 80 miles a hour, scattering pedestrians as they went, and screeching round police cars that tried to slow them down. The Prince was predictably furious.

Diana's arrival with the children a couple of days later cheered him up considerably, as did being surrounded by so many friends. King Constantine was

Charles was cheered to be surrounded by family and friends on their Majorcan holiday in 1990

holidaying with them, and also the Romseys with their children; but Charles was still in a certain amount of pain, and frustrated and impatient at being unable to do anything physical. He could not swim; he could not even use his right hand to write or to paint.

When he returned home at the end of the holiday, he had a routine X-ray to see how the arm was healing; this discovered that although the uppermost of the two fractures had mended well, the lower break had not.

His doctors decided to operate. So on 31 August the Prince was taken into the Queen's Medical Centre in Nottingham, a National Health Service hospital, to be operated on next day by two of the country's leading specialists in the field, Mr John Webb and Mr Christopher Colton. It was a gruelling three-hour operation, which involved chipping away fragments of bone from his hip, inserting a metal plate into his arm to join the broken pieces and packing the bone chips around the join. Diana was at the hospital with him; she was there for thirteen hours that day, and stayed with friends in the neighbourhood so she could be near at hand.

It was a worrying time for her, yet while he was under the anaesthetic, she went visiting the wards to bring a bit of cheer; it emerged some weeks later that she had been particularly solicitous of a young man who was in a coma as a result of a motorcycle accident. His parents said it was the Princess who had brought him out of it. She had sat with him, held his hand and talked to him and had, they said, miraculously brought him back to them.

With the operation over, the most important part of his treatment was yet to come: the physiotherapy. He had called on an Australian physiotherapist, forty-one-year-old Sarah Key, who had treated a back injury of the Prince's some years before, and she started the course of treatment while he was still under the anaesthetic on the operating table. He was told that if he ever wanted to have full use of the arm again and be fit enough to ride horses, he would have to follow a punishing course of painful exercises. Charles embarked on them with an icy determination to succeed, and pushed himself to the limit every day.

He was in hospital for just over a week, having regular sessions with Sarah Key; in between times, he worked. He had set up an office in an adjoining room at the

Diana and the boys visit Charles in hospital in Nottingham after his three-hour operation

hospital, where members of his staff installed themselves, with a direct telephone link to Buckingham Palace, to handle, among other things, the torrent of mail that arrived for the Prince and get-well messages from the general public. The doctors had said that he should carry out no engagements for six to ten weeks, so he was persuaded that rather than cancel a few of the obviously strenuous things, he should cancel everything to the end of October. Worried as she was about the pain he was in, Diana remained bright and cheerful. She came to visit frequently, and brought William and Harry to see their father too. Charles was putting on a brave face, but was very uncomfortable.

On 10 September they all had to put on a brave face. It was Prince William's first day at boarding school, and a mighty wrench, especially for Diana. It had been inevitable that he would go away to school at eight. It was not only the most practical solution to his education; it was what most little boys in their social stratum do, and it would have been very surprising if he had not. They had chosen the school with care, after looking at a number of other prep schools, because it was a friendly family school and they liked the atmosphere. It was nevertheless very upsetting saying goodbye, and the weekend of William's first exeat, 29 September, was written in letters of fire in Diana's diary, a day to be kept free at all costs.

With William installed at school, Charles flew off to Provence in the south of

France to recuperate at the château of an old friend, taking Sarah Key with him. The doctors had prescribed sunshine, warmth and a swimming pool, in which he could exercise his arm. It was also thought that being away from his desk, and the temptation to work, might give the wound a better chance of healing. It was good in theory, but the press had become preoccupied by his health. There were daily reports, and suggestions that his arm had become infected after the 'second operation' (showing that they were unaware that the first had simply been manipulation). Questions were even asked in the House of Commons about the Prince's condition.

To his inestimable fury, the press found his hideaway. He climbed out of bed one morning, put on a dressing gown, and opened up the curtains in his bedroom to find a bank of photographers camped on a handy hillside opposite. Standing well back from the window, he stared at them, gloomily wondering what kind of day it was going to be with zoom lenses pointing at him as he exercised in the sun, unaware that at that very moment those zoom lenses were focusing on him as clearly as if he had been posing two feet away.

From France he went to Balmoral, to the therapeutic calm of the Highlands, where the press counted the days and the weeks that he and Diana were apart with ever more ominous comment. Why was he not choosing the comfort of his family instead of solitude 500 miles away? Why had he not even returned for William's first weekend out from school? Whenever he was sighted he looked irritable and glum. Was he having a nervous breakdown? Was the marriage falling apart?

The answer was no. His choice of the Highlands over home was hardly cause for concern, when he has spent the best part of the autumn there without his wife and children for the last seven years. As usual, he had invited friends up to do some stalking, long before his accident, and he did not want to put them off. He also wanted to spend some time with the Queen Mother, at Birkhall, as he does every autumn. It is the only chance he gets to see her for a significant period. And what the doctor ordered was exercise: long walks to keep the hip moving.

The operation had knocked him for six. He had expected to feel as he did after the first stay in hospital, but three and a half hours under anaesthetic had seriously dented his reserves. He was also in a considerable amount of pain – not so much from the arm, but from the hip which had had flakes of bone chipped away from it. The physiotherapy was painful too. And the timing could not have been worse. Just as everything was coming together, exciting new projects starting up, others reaching fruition, he was knocked out of action. All the credibility that he had built up with the press was suddenly wiped out. They were back to the same tired old themes.

It was intensely frustrating. Four months' worth of engagements had been erased from his diary, including a four-day trip to Brazil with the Princess at the end of October, which he had been eagerly looking forward to. After what promised to be a fascinating visit in itself, he and Brazil's President Collor had planned a twenty-four-hour seminar on board *Britannia* on the subject of sustainable development, with a select group of twenty international figures. The trip would be rescheduled, but the diary had now been worked out for the next six months and there would not be time until way into the New Year. There were other engagements that could never be reconvened.

Normally such frustrations would have been worked out on the polo field. That was where he exorcised his anger and the pent-up stresses and strains of the job; it was there that he let off steam, and came away fresh and, as he has said himself, 'five hundred times better in my mental outlook'. Without some kind of sport there was no channel for releasing those emotions. In addition to which, sport was something of an addiction. As any serious sportsman or sportswoman will attest, hard physical exercise produces an unmistakable feeling of euphoria, sometimes referred to as 'runner's high', caused by a release of endorphins, which the body craves in much the same way as it craves any other substance it is addicted to when it is withdrawn, such as cigarettes or alcohol.

But as time passed and his body recovered from the trauma of surgery, he became very much happier. He managed to get a tremendous amount of work done, which he could never have achieved in London. Being in Scotland he could control who came to see him, and he was not pressured into doing things as he would have been at home. For the first time in five years he had a completely clear desk – if only for one day. He wrote a number of speeches that he was particularly pleased with while he was there, and recorded some of them on video. He also became involved in some local issues, and invited a group of interested parties to Balmoral to discuss problems such as footpath erosion, tourism, vandalism and the national parks.

Far from being gloomy and on the point of cracking up, people who were with him say they had seldom seen the Prince look brighter. When he returned to the fray on the last day of October, appropriately to visit the holistic Marylebone Medical Centre in London, he was cheerful and relaxed. He could manage an army salute with his right arm and scratch the back of his neck, and he had plans to do some gentle hunting after Christmas. A skiing holiday was already in the diary, and so was a season full of polo matches for 1991, including a benefit match for the two hospitals that had treated him. The patient was much, much better.

Portrait of a Marriage

No two married couples have the same sort of marriage. There are some who rely 100 per cent on each other, who cannot function properly without their other half and who feel bereft and inadequate if they are on their own for any time at all. There are others who spend months apart – the husband away on contract work in the oilfields or at sea in the Navy, whose wives bring up the children and run the house – yet whose relationship is kept alive by the excitement of seeing each other again. And there are hundreds of thousands of marriages in which the husband leaves home at the crack of dawn to commute to work, when the rest of the household are still asleep, and is not back until after the children are in bed at night. At the weekend he is off playing golf or watching football. Such families may all live under the same roof 365 days a year, but for all they see of one another they could be miles away. What works for one couple sounds like purgatory for another. There are mixes of age, race and creed in some relationships that other people could never countenance.

Charles and Diana have a marriage that works for them. Given the pressure they have had to live with and the difficulties they have had, it is something of a miracle, but there is no doubt their union is strong and permanent and that they love one another very deeply – no longer so passionately as they did when they were honey-mooners, but with the familiarity and affection of two horses who have spent ten years working in harness. Their relationship is all the better for periods apart – as are dozens of relationships.

Their children are secure and confident, happy at school, and cheerful and bouncy little boys at home. Their parents may be away more than some, but they are hardly 'latch-key kids'; they have a house full of adults they know and love, they dart in and out of every room as they please, and there is not a single member of staff at either Highgrove or Kensington Palace who is not utterly enchanted by them both. When Charles and Diana are at home, they get far more attention from their parents than many a child does from parents who are at home all the time.

It is impossible for any ordinary man to appreciate fully the work-load, the responsibility and the sense of duty that drive the Prince. There are tycoons who are driven to wheel and deal and amass greater fortunes and greater empires (whose

families probably see far less of them than the Prince's), there are politicians who desperately battle for their beliefs, who try to influence and improve society (who also probably see less of their family than the Prince), but none of these people have the combination of forces at work that Charles does. They do not have the feeling of responsibility that he has; the need constantly to prove himself; to keep within the constraints of the Constitution; and to have every word, thought and deed subjected to public scrutiny.

One man in a similar position is his cousin and friend, King Constantine of Greece. He is in exile, but he still shoulders the burden of responsibility for the citizens he was forced to leave behind, and for others in exile. His work takes him all over the world, and he too spends long periods away from his family, because duty comes before personal pleasure; but even he says that the Prince's dedication to his work is phenomenal, his desire to pay back to society the privilege it has afforded him.

There is no single figure one can compare with Diana. The stresses she lives with and faces in her public life are hard to envisage, but each day is another challenge, another performance, another terror. Diana was not born to it; she has embraced duty of her own volition, with the same warmth and sensitivity that the Queen Mother did. There is no good reason why she could not have quietly settled down to life as a wife and mother. She is not paid by the civil list – technically, she owes the nation nothing. There is no need to stand up and speak, and half scare herself to death in the process. Yet she takes on an exhausting schedule. Take just two days last October; on Tuesday, 22 October, she was in Portsmouth. During three hours and twenty-one minutes precisely, she visited six different sites, unveiled four plaques, cut two cakes, and ceremoniously set a stone for the new part of the cathedral.

At 10.54 a.m. precisely a great cheer went up from the crowd as a bright-red Wessex helicopter appeared in the sky; it was at first only the faintest dot, but it gradually grew bigger and louder as the great red beast came down to land on the netball courts of Milton School, in Southsea, a suburb of Portsmouth. Hundreds of people, dozens of them children, had been standing waiting for this moment for two hours or more. Policemen anxiously paced up and down the lines of people cordoned off behind rope barriers, their eyes darting through the crowds, alert for trouble. They had begun making the area 'sterile' at 7 a.m., when the sniffer dogs went in. The road outside had been cleared and the whole area was filled with uniformed policemen, all wearing or carrying gloves, as they traditionally do for royal visits. A white van pulled up outside, and immediately a chief inspector dispatched a constable to find out who it belonged to and move it on. The only vehicles allowed in the road were the official cars, a black and grey Daimler that would carry the Princess and her lady-in-waiting, a white BMW belonging to the local police force as escort, a green Royalty Protection Squad Rover for Diana's personal detective and equerry, and a fleet of motorcycle outriders. Also in the street was the minibus laid on for the rota press party.

The Princess stepped out of the helicopter and was greeted by the Lord Lieutenant

No two marriages are the same. Charles and Diana at Royal Ascot

It is a big extended family – the boys are hardly 'latch-key kids'. With the Queen at Sandringham, 1988

of Hampshire, who presented his wife to her; the Lord Mayor of Portsmouth and his wife; the leader of the city council and his wife; the chief executive and his wife; and the deputy chief constable – a formidable troop, just the first of many she was to encounter in the course of the day. By the time she left that first venue, a small building, she had had formally presented to her no fewer than twenty-five dignitaries and countless people who used the centre, including a group of dancers who put on a display for the Princess.

What she clearly enjoyed most though was meeting ordinary people. At every stop, she headed straight for the crowds contained behind the cordons, smiled warmly, said good morning to everyone, and shook hands with each and every hand she could reach. She did not go past a wheelchair without stopping, she bent down to talk to children, accepted posies and scruffy home-made offerings, and laughed at remarks people made. From the crowd she took a hand reaching up from below, which she took to be a child's. When she looked down, it was no child, but a fully grown dwarf grinning up at her, saying, 'That fooled you, didn't it?' The Princess burst out laughing and blushed to the roots, and confessed she was right; but she was not caught out again. The woman appeared at every location that day and, to her immense delight, at each place Diana spotted her among the crowd and laughed.

There were serious moments in the course of the day too. The second stop was a day centre for homeless families, some of whom looked very down on their luck. Diana sat down with them and asked about their circumstances and how they managed to cope, and sympathized with their problems. After a centenary buffet lunch at the Guildhall, where she cut the first of her cakes, Portsmouth's most senior citizen, 107-year-old Mrs Bessie Thomas, was presented to her. She was in a wheel-chair. Immediately Diana cupped the old lady's hand in hers and squatted down beside her, shooing away a chair that was quickly brought for her to sit on.

At other times she was more frivolous. She wore the look of one who never got things quite right. The sword she was supposed to cut the centenary cake with didn't glide gracefully through it. She pulled the wrong curtain cord on three out of four of the plaques she unveiled, so the curtain didn't open when everyone expected it to; and the one time she got it right, she was so surprised that she blushed and giggled. At the cathedral she gave the foundation stone such a wallop that everyone gasped thinking the stone might crack, and the bishop had to tell her to be a little more gentle at the next hit. Every time she would pull a face and giggle, or bite her lip, put her hand to her mouth, and look wide-eyed and little-girlish; a brilliant ploy, which made everyone instantly adore her, and made all the men feel positively protective towards her.

But her *tour de force* was with children at an adventure playground in Portsea, where they kept animals such as goats, guinea pigs and rabbits. Without hesitation, Diana went straight over to a group of tough-looking children, aged between about eight and thirteen, sitting in a not-unthreatening way on top of a climbing frame. She put one foot up on the bottom bar, wrapped her arms around one of the upright bars, and began to talk to them. Their hostility gradually evaporated, and they became animated and giggly. Although dressed in an immaculate cream suit, she squatted down to let a big black rabbit sit in her lap, then a guinea pig, and she talked to the goat. And she took more and more animals in her arms as children queued up to present them to her for inspection.

'Gosh, that one's a bit fat, isn't it?' she said, taking hold of an outsize model.

'That's because it's expecting babies,' said a little girl.

'Oh dear,' said Diana, blushing. 'I rather asked for that.'

She then went and sat down on a piece of play equipment, and six or seven little girls sat with her, one of whom she hoisted on to her lap. She put her arm around another and stroked the child's pony tail, as she answered all their questions and showed them her engagement ring, which they were dying to see. 'You could buy a few rabbits with that,' she said, laughing. Where was Prince Charles, they wanted to know, and why had she not brought Prince William and Prince Harry with her? The Prince was in Scotland, she explained, and the children were at school. Did they like Teenage Mutant Hero Turtles, and were they going to get the video? 'They're going to get it for Christmas,' said Diana, 'provided they work hard and get good reports from school.'

From there the Princess was whisked off to HMS *Nelson* for a five-minute stop, then away. It was a hectic schedule and at the end of the day she must have been exhausted, everyone else certainly was – and they had done none of the hand shaking and small talk, they had not been ogled at and scrutinized, they had not had to remember who everyone was and what everyone did, knowing that one gaff would be front-page news. Yet Diana went on to a dinner engagement in Portsmouth before flying back to Kensington Palace for the night.

The next morning, she began all over again. A Wessex helicopter landed at St Augustine's Hospital in Chartham in Kent at 10.50. She was greeted by the Deputy Lord Lieutenant of Kent, who presented the chief constable, the Mayor of Canterbury, the chief executive, the local MP, and so it went on throughout another day: the ubiquitous string of dignitaries and their wives. St Augustine's is an old Victorian psychiatric hospital, which is in the process of being decommissioned, and the point of the Kent visit was principally to attend a mental-health seminar organized by Turning Point, St Augustine's and the private Priory Hospitals Group, to discuss the difficulties and opportunities presented to the three sectors – voluntary, NHS and private – by the government's new Community Care Act. After speeches from the three parties involved, there was a question-and-answer session and discussion.

Beforehand, Diana had visited residents in three wards of the hospital, one for continuing care, where the patients were engaged in recreational activities, and she cut a cake in celebration of the visit; one for disturbed people; and a third for acute admissions.

From there she went to Ashford for a quick forty-minute stop, to open a new building for a perfume company that had donated £1,000 to Turning Point, look over its manufacturing departments and unveil a plaque, before flying on to the Tenterden Leisure Centre. She whizzed round here in forty-five minutes, chatted and joked with a party of disabled swimmers in the pool, and also a mother and toddler group, and officially declared the building open with yet another plaque. From there she flew straight back to Kensington Palace and was back in time for tea with Prince Harry, before starting all over again the next day.

Rushed as the schedules are, the only people who notice how little time she spends anywhere are the Princess, her aides and the police, for whom such visits are a major security problem. The members of the public who meet her, whose hands she clasps, whose questions she answers, have no such memory. For them it is quite simply an experience of a lifetime.

'How's Prince Charles's arm?' asked one woman outside the Guildhall in Portsmouth.

'It's much better, thank you,' said Diana.

'Are you going to make him stop playing polo now?' she said.

'No,' said Diana. 'You must never stop a man doing what he wants to do.'

It was the secret of her success in a nutshell. What she has created for Charles is a secure base, a warm, comfortable, happy home that he can come and go from, as his work, his sports and his whims take him, without having to explain or justify himself. Diana, meanwhile, gets on with her life, her work, her friends, the children, and with all her various hobbies and sports. When they have time to spend together it is an enormous pleasure to them both. She has learned a lot in the last ten years, so has Charles; it has not been an easy time for either of them, but they have come through it. They have a marriage that is all the stronger for having had its problems, and one that will see them safely into the future with all the change and uncertainty that lie ahead.

Charles and Diana in Cameroon

Overleaf *Charles and Diana together in Japan for the enthronement of the Emperor*